M000268284

The Viking Gods

The Viking Gods

Pagan Myths of Nordic Peoples

Clive Barrett

THE AQUARIAN PRESS

First published 1989

© CLIVE BARRETT 1989

All rights reserved. No part of this book may be reproduced or utilized in any form or by any means, electronic or mechanical, including photocopying, recording or by any information storage and retrieval system, without permission in writing from the Publisher.

British Library Cataloguing in Publication Data

Barrett, Clive
The Viking gods
1. Norse myths
I. Title
293.13

ISBN 0-85030-775-9

The Aquarian Press is part of the Thorsons Publishing Group, Wellingborough, Northamptonshire, NN8 2RQ, England

Typeset by Harper Phototypesetters Limited, Northampton, England.
Printed in Great Britain by Butler & Tanner Limited, Frome, Somerset

1 3 5 7 9 10 8 6 4 2

contents

introduction

T he origin of the Viking myths lies lost in the depths of time. They appear to have their roots amongst the ancient group of peoples known collectively as Indo-European. The myths, in a form still recognizable today however, grew and developed in the region populated by the Germanic tribes and later extended into Scandinavia.

Following the fall of the Roman Empire these barbarian tribes migrated across northern and western Europe taking their beliefs with them. The Angles came to southern Britain, giving it the name Angleland or England, followed by the Jutes and Saxons. Together these peoples brought an age of paganism to a land which, under the protection of the Roman armies, had been Christian for roughly a hundred years. They brought the myths of Odin and of Thor to the fearful Christian Celts. As time passed however, the newcomers were themselves converted, by various means, to Christianity by the missionaries and the indigenous population.

The return of Christianity was short-lived, for in the eighth century the Vikings came to these British shores. In 793 they attacked St Cuthbert's monastery at Lindisfarne and from then on they plundered coastal towns as and when they wished. Later the Norsemen began to settle, first in the Hebrides, the Orkneys and the Isle of Man, then finally

in the 860s they began to colonize much of northern and eastern England. Following a treaty with Alfred the Great in the year 878, the whole of this area, that is the land above a rough line from the river Lea to the river Dee, came firmly under the rule of the pagan kings.

There followed a period of continual unrest between the Saxons and the Norsemen. Slowly with the ascendancy of the Kingdom of Wessex the power of the northern kings waned, until by the middle of the tenth century the English had reconquered the lost areas. But early in the eleventh century the whole of England was again conquered by the Vikings, and in 1016, King Canute, a Danish Viking, was accepted as king of all England.

After the death of Canute and his sons, rulership returned to the Saxons, and in 1042 Edward the Confessor became king. He was succeeded in 1066 by the ill-fated Harold Godwinson, who first fought off an invading army of Vikings at Stamford Bridge, but was finally defeated at Hastings by the forces of the Normans, who were themselves descended from the Norsemen.

From the time of the departure of the Romans early in the fifth century, England was constantly under the rule of a group of related peoples originated from northern Germany and Scandinavia. As a result, each new influx of pagans brought with it beliefs which were already familiar to the existing inhabitants of England. The country swayed precariously between Christianity and paganism, finally falling towards Christianity after the defeat of the Vikings in 1066.

Throughout the whole of this period (and still later) Christianity bore a marked resemblance to their former pagan beliefs. Remnants of this remain visible today, the carvings upon stone crosses and elsewhere show a mixture

of pagan and Christian belief. In one such carving Balder, the Norse god of light and wisdom, is clearly equated with Christ. A mould has also been discovered which was used for casting both small metal hammer talismans and Christian crosses side by side.

In order to gain acceptance for their cause, the Christian missionaries emphasized similarities between the two faiths and actively encouraged a form of dual worship. It was for this reason that many early churches were founded on sites of traditional pagan worship. The missionaries had a great advantage over the Northern priests in that they were organized and, with both threats of Hell and promises of Heaven, they actively sought converts to their faith. The pagan priests, however, were independent and unorganized by their very nature, and further were happy to let any man believe whatever he wished. These factors greatly contributed to the eventual supremacy of Christianity over the former beliefs of the north.

Today we cannot hope to understand completely just what the myths meant to the Northern peoples. Our beliefs, ideals and moral standards are so far removed from those of our ancestors that we are unable to fully comprehend the part the gods played in their daily lives.

The religion of the North was not an homogeneous whole,

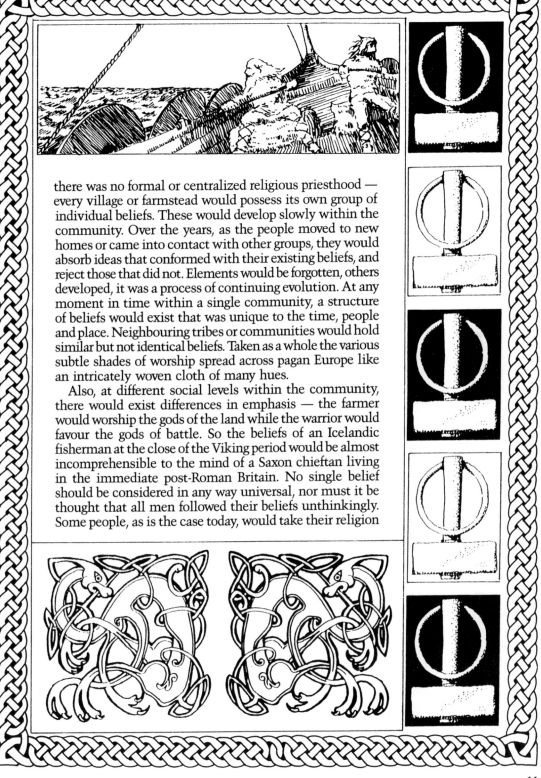

there was no formal or centralized religious priesthood — every village or farmstead would possess its own group of individual beliefs. These would develop slowly within the community. Over the years, as the people moved to new homes or came into contact with other groups, they would absorb ideas that conformed with their existing beliefs, and reject those that did not. Elements would be forgotten, others developed, it was a process of continuing evolution. At any moment in time within a single community, a structure of beliefs would exist that was unique to the time, people and place. Neighbouring tribes or communities would hold similar but not identical beliefs. Taken as a whole the various subtle shades of worship spread across pagan Europe like an intricately woven cloth of many hues.

Also, at different social levels within the community, there would exist differences in emphasis — the farmer would worship the gods of the land while the warrior would favour the gods of battle. So the beliefs of an Icelandic fisherman at the close of the Viking period would be almost incomprehensible to the mind of a Saxon chieftan living in the immediate post-Roman Britain. No single belief should be considered in any way universal, nor must it be thought that all men followed their beliefs unthinkingly. Some people, as is the case today, would take their religion

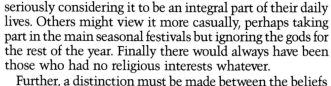

seriously considering it to be an integral part of their daily lives. Others might view it more casually, perhaps taking part in the main seasonal festivals but ignoring the gods for the rest of the year. Finally there would always have been those who had no religious interests whatever.

Further, a distinction must be made between the beliefs of the people and the mythologies of poets. The poets were professional entertainers, and it is from them that we gain most of our knowledge of the Northern myths. The myths were created in an illiterate society. Although later the use of written runes became widespread, they were used only for short inscriptions and not for recording the lengthy myths. Their stories were handed from generation to generation, passing down the centuries by word of mouth. To aid in the accurate transfer and to help the poets and skalds memorize the material, the stories were presented within an elaborately structured poetry. This stylized form, forever seeking new and novel components, invited the use of alien mythological sources, and the poets borrowed freely from Mediterranean and Eastern sources. After the end of the pagan period the poets continued to use their mythological material developing it along Christian lines and providing the stories with morals acceptable to the rapidly growing church.

It is from these later works that much of our knowledge of the Northern myths is derived. They are the work of Christian writers. In the twelfth century the Dane Saxo Grammaticus wrote a history of Denmark, the first nine parts of which contain a wealth of pagan material. It is evident that he had little love for the subject, and found many of the legends extremely distasteful. However he does preserve material that would otherwise have been lost.

Another writer to record the pagan myths was the Icelander Snorri Sturluson (1172-1241), who was a poet, historian and politician. Seeing that the native traditions were losing ground, around the year 1220 he wrote a handbook for poets, known as the *Younger* or *Prose Edda*. He provided them with instructions on the recognition of allusions within the myths and their correct poetic use. His writings are based upon oral traditions, some of which can be found in the *Poetic Edda*, along with others which are no longer known; indeed he quotes from some 17 lost mythological poems. Throughout his work he shows a sympathy and enthusiasm for the myths, which is remarkable for a man of his time, retelling the tales with skill and originality, and as a result his versions of the legends are usually preferred to those of Saxo Grammaticus. However, when he was writing, Christianity had enjoyed

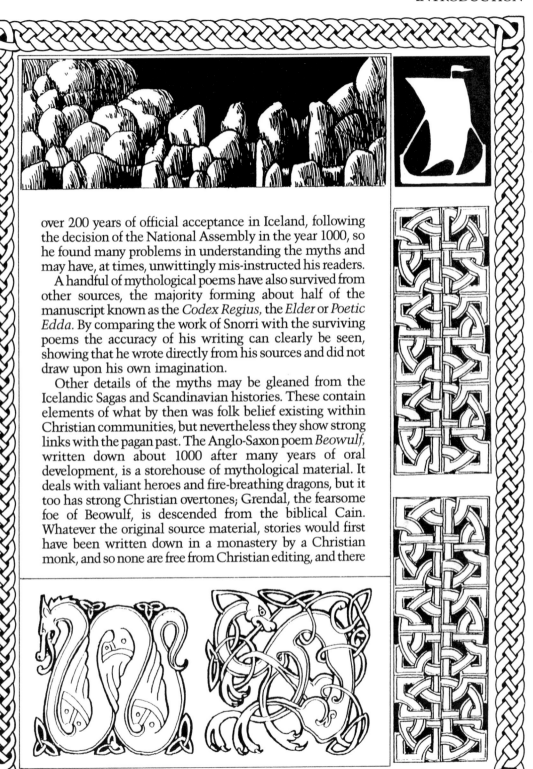

over 200 years of official acceptance in Iceland, following the decision of the National Assembly in the year 1000, so he found many problems in understanding the myths and may have, at times, unwittingly mis-instructed his readers.

A handful of mythological poems have also survived from other sources, the majority forming about half of the manuscript known as the *Codex Regius*, the *Elder* or *Poetic Edda*. By comparing the work of Snorri with the surviving poems the accuracy of his writing can clearly be seen, showing that he wrote directly from his sources and did not draw upon his own imagination.

Other details of the myths may be gleaned from the Icelandic Sagas and Scandinavian histories. These contain elements of what by then was folk belief existing within Christian communities, but nevertheless they show strong links with the pagan past. The Anglo-Saxon poem *Beowulf*, written down about 1000 after many years of oral development, is a storehouse of mythological material. It deals with valiant heroes and fire-breathing dragons, but it too has strong Christian overtones; Grendal, the fearsome foe of Beowulf, is descended from the biblical Cain. Whatever the original source material, stories would first have been written down in a monastery by a Christian monk, and so none are free from Christian editing, and there

can be no doubt that many legends were omitted or discarded completely.

Archaeologists may at times shed new light upon the myths. From excavating Anglo-Saxon cemeteries, finds in the form of small hammers have provided evidence that the worship of the god Thor outlasted that of the other gods. This has to be balanced against the humorous treatment of Thor in the later myths. Had his power waned to such an extent that he became a figure of fun, or was he still highly revered?

The myths as we have received them are incomplete, they are only the ragged remnants of a once-glorious tradition. Some stories, it is true, are rich and full of wonderful detail. But many more are known only in a heavily condensed form often consisting of no more than a few lines of text. Some are brief in the extreme, others confused and self-contradicting, nevertheless they are still of immense value. From these imperfect and scattered fragments we are able to assemble a faint glimmer of a rich and varied mythology, the beliefs that prevailed throughout northern Europe for over a thousand years.

As with the written sources of Northern myths our knowledge of the history and people of the period is also drawn from the works of not impartial Christian scribes. However, with this in mind and using information contained in the later Sagas, it is possible to draw an accurate picture of Viking life.

While the Norseman would defend his personal freedom and independence to the death if necessary, he also placed great emphasis on the importance of family life and ties. The family acted as a strong and single unit, each member secure in the knowledge that every other member would support and assist him in times of need. If a man failed in his obligations, then he risked being cast out from his family, and being denied the benefit of their support. To stand alone against the uncertainties of the world, with no hope of help from any man, brought fear to the strongest heart. This led men to cultivate friendships, for although a man would have his family to back him up in a dispute, the opposing family might be equally strong and powerful. Thus an ill-chosen word or an ill-conceived action could, as described to great effect in Egil's Saga, easily escalate into the most tragic sequence of retaliation and counter-retaliation.

In the past life was hard, men had to be able to stand up to all that might be set against them. There were three basic avenues of work available to which a Norseman could turn

in order to sustain himself and his family. These were farming by growing crops or raising animals, hunting and fishing, and trading. In reality the majority of men would engage in more than one of these, depending on local circumstances.

The sea offered fish, the fertile plains provided great scope for arable farming, while the mountain pastures encouraged the herding of sheep. Full advantage was taken of any opportunity that presented itself — a man might easily be farmer, fisherman, hunter and trader.

In all these occupations there was a strong element of uncertainty. The farmer and the fisherman relied much upon favourable weather. Without sun and rain in the correct season or the benefit of a good wind when required all his efforts were doomed to failure. In addition to being dependent upon the weather, the trader, if he chose to travel in search of profit, also had to contend with the lawless bands of pirates who swarmed the seas in search of easy plunder.

The womenfolk would work in the fields with their husbands or about the home. They would spin and weave cloth (although this was not an occupation reserved wholly for women), cook and attend to the domestic side of life. They had equal rites in marriage and were given equal say in the running of the household. They also held the keys of the house, which along with small knives and other useful implements, were suspended on chains either from their waists or from a decorative brooch.

So with his family firmly behind him, a man faced what was essentially an unfriendly and unpredictable world. In this unsure climate, two things developed hand in hand. The first was a healthy ambivalence to the problems of life. Life passed too quickly to dwell on its shortcomings — it was

lived to the full, each day taken as it came. Even in the depths of disaster one should retain hope and a cheerful heart. The greatest of enemies held in highest esteem those who met death with a joke on their lips. The second development was a collection of myths and legends which fully reflect the nature of life, peopled by gods who had themselves little control over their own futures. Susceptible to ageing and the passage of time, their lives lay in the hands of a force more powerful than themselves. They could be killed like mortals — even Odin, the god of war and death, could not be totally relied upon to provide his followers with victory, nor could he bring his much-loved son back from the dead.

The nature of the gods falls into two distinct categories. There were the gods of war, sky and justice, and the gods of the earth and fertility. The former were the Aesir, the warrior gods of Asgard, and the latter the Vanir of Vanaheim. It was to the gods and goddesses of the Vanir that the farmer and the hunter turned for assistance. Niord, the leader of the Vanir, was the god of both fertility and the sea. His son Freyr possessed a magical ship and was also concerned with fertility. He was ruler of Alfheim, land of the elves, those helpful spirits of the earth. Freya, Niord's daughter, was the goddess of love and beauty, who presided over childbirth.

Of the Aesir we have Odin the sky god, the god of war, sacrifice and runes. Tyr was an older sky god whose place Odin had assumed. Then there is Forseti, the god of law and justice, and Bragi, god of poetry and music. These were all gods of people of a higher social class; the ordinary man had little time for such matters as concerned the Aesir. Also of the Aesir, but standing apart from them in her sphere of concern, is Frigga, the wife of Odin. Her attributes were so similar to those of Freya that one cannot avoid coming to the conclusion that the two were derived from a common

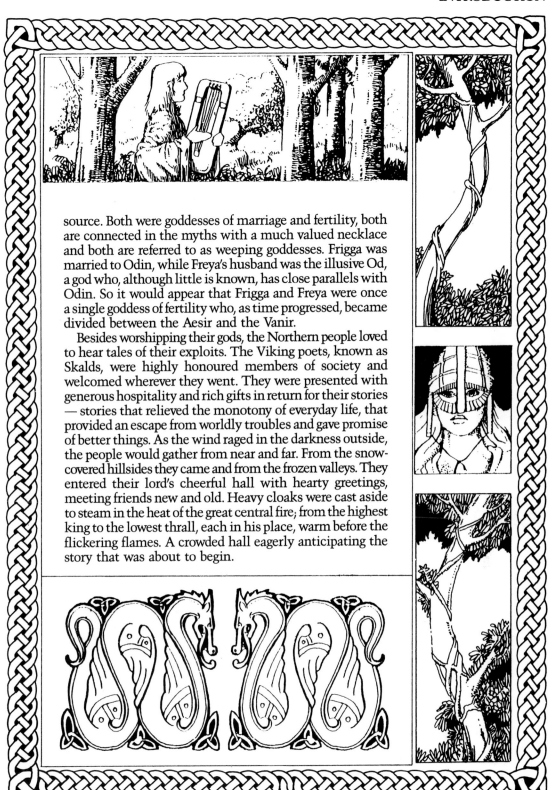

source. Both were goddesses of marriage and fertility, both are connected in the myths with a much valued necklace and both are referred to as weeping goddesses. Frigga was married to Odin, while Freya's husband was the illusive Od, a god who, although little is known, has close parallels with Odin. So it would appear that Frigga and Freya were once a single goddess of fertility who, as time progressed, became divided between the Aesir and the Vanir.

Besides worshipping their gods, the Northern people loved to hear tales of their exploits. The Viking poets, known as Skalds, were highly honoured members of society and welcomed wherever they went. They were presented with generous hospitality and rich gifts in return for their stories — stories that relieved the monotony of everyday life, that provided an escape from worldly troubles and gave promise of better things. As the wind raged in the darkness outside, the people would gather from near and far. From the snow-covered hillsides they came and from the frozen valleys. They entered their lord's cheerful hall with hearty greetings, meeting friends new and old. Heavy cloaks were cast aside to steam in the heat of the great central fire; from the highest king to the lowest thrall, each in his place, warm before the flickering flames. A crowded hall eagerly anticipating the story that was about to begin.

the first gods

N o earth, no heaven, no rock, sea or sand. At the very dawn of time, there was nothing. No warming sun, no shimmering moon, no stars above. Nothing but the unseen expanse of Ginnungagap. The black abyss of chaos.

Many ages passed and the chaos stirred and heaved. To the South there gradually became a dim glow in the blackness, flickering faintly at first, then burning brighter and yet brighter. So arrived the red world of fire, Muspell, whose environs were lethal to all but its inhabitants. Sitting brooding on the boundary of Muspell was Surtur, the mighty being, armed with a flaming sword, guarding his world of fire until the end of time. In the final hours of the earth he will rise from his seat and come forth to destroy the gods and devour the universe with flame.

To the North there was a world of clouds and shadow called Niflheim, at whose heart lay the spring Hvergelmir. From this fathomless cauldron flowed the Elivagar, the 12 great dark rivers of Niflheim. As they progressed they became colder, and one by one the rivers began to freeze. The ice that formed on their surface was pushed along by the force of the flow. Blocks of ice ground against each other, they were crushed and smashed under the growing pressure only to freeze once again in ever more bizarre shapes and forms. Onward the river of thundering ice rolled, onward until it cascaded down into the roaring depths of Ginnungagap.

From the South sped rivers of flame and venom. In time they too hardened, becoming a solid glowing mass of embers, just as lava solidifies on its descent from the volcano. At the place where the rivers of ice and fire met, a noxious mist arose, billowing upwards for a time before freezing once more to form hoarfrost on the vast surface.

And so, as the aeons passed, the abyss began to fill. In the Northern part of Ginnungagap there was a region of ice-storms and wind-driven snow, while in the South there was

a realm of glowing heat, lit by the sparks and flames that flowed from Muspelheim. In the centre, a place of peace and calm where these extremes met and cancelled themselves out, a balance was found. When the snows of the North met the warming breezes of the South, drops of rain began to fall. These drops joined and took shape to become human in appearance. The creature formed was Ymir, the first of the race of frost giants (Hrimthursar). They called him Orgelmir.

Following Ymir, more ice melted and took the shape of a giant cow called Aurgelmir. Groping about in the dim light searching for food, Ymir found her and was gladdened to discover that from her udder flowed four streams of rich milk. His hunger was then satisfied and Ymir slept, but Aurgelmir in turn looked for food. She licked at the ice around her and finding the salty taste pleasing she continued to lick. After a time the hair of a god could be seen upon the ice, then as she licked his head was exposed from its frosty casing. Eventually, after three long days, to the sound of Ymir's echoing snores and Aurgelmir's licking tongue, Buri stepped forth, free at last, from his chilled cage of ice.

Still Ymir slept. He began to perspire and from the pit of his left arm came a man and a woman, then from his legs sprang a giant named Thrudgelmir. Shortly after his own

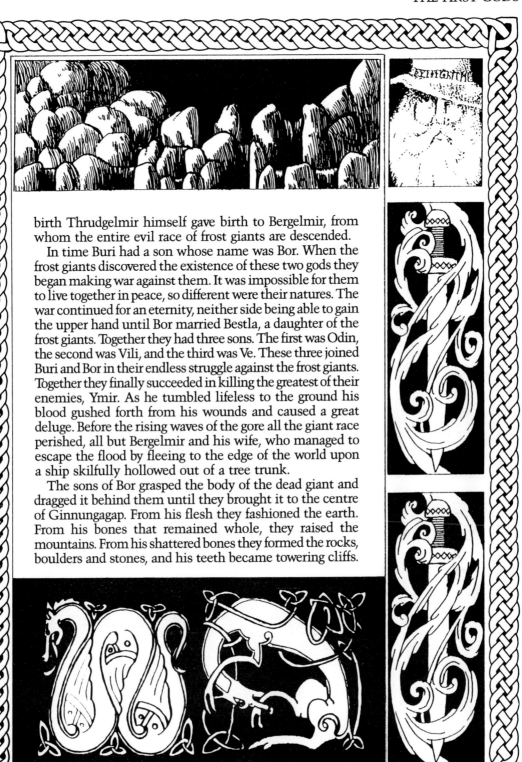

birth Thrudgelmir himself gave birth to Bergelmir, from whom the entire evil race of frost giants are descended.

In time Buri had a son whose name was Bor. When the frost giants discovered the existence of these two gods they began making war against them. It was impossible for them to live together in peace, so different were their natures. The war continued for an eternity, neither side being able to gain the upper hand until Bor married Bestla, a daughter of the frost giants. Together they had three sons. The first was Odin, the second was Vili, and the third was Ve. These three joined Buri and Bor in their endless struggle against the frost giants. Together they finally succeeded in killing the greatest of their enemies, Ymir. As he tumbled lifeless to the ground his blood gushed forth from his wounds and caused a great deluge. Before the rising waves of the gore all the giant race perished, all but Bergelmir and his wife, who managed to escape the flood by fleeing to the edge of the world upon a ship skilfully hollowed out of a tree trunk.

The sons of Bor grasped the body of the dead giant and dragged it behind them until they brought it to the centre of Ginnungagap. From his flesh they fashioned the earth. From his bones that remained whole, they raised the mountains. From his shattered bones they formed the rocks, boulders and stones, and his teeth became towering cliffs.

His curling hair became the trees and plants upon the earth. As his swirling blood stilled, the ocean that surrounds the earth was born.

The gods took his great skull and balanced it above the earth, resting in the strong hands of four dwarfs. The dwarfs stood at the four corners of the earth and they named them Nordri, Sudri, Austri and Westri. Into this cavernous dome they cast Ymir's brains to become the clouds of the sky. But their world was dark and unlit so the gods sought the bright sparks and red-hot flames from Muspelheim. Gathering a great number together they scattered them across the sky above, where they shone down into the gloom as stars, each set in its appointed position or traversing its prescribed course in the heavenly vault.

The brightest of these sparks they put aside and from them they created the sun and the moon. Taking their new creations they set them in chariots of gold. To the chariot of the sun they harnessed two horses, Arvakr (the early waker) and Alsvin (the rapid goer). Afraid that the animals should suffer from the burning heat of the sphere, the gods set upon the front of the chariot the shield Svalin (the cooler) without which both the horses and the earth would have been burned to ash. Likewise the chariot of the moon was harnessed to a third horse, Alsvider (the allswift), but he required no shield to protect him from the sharp but cool rays of the moon.

Around the earth the gods raised a wall against the troublesome giants made from the eyebrows of Ymir. This land within the wall they named Midgard, the Middle Earth.

One day the sons of Bor were walking together along the sea shore between the grey rocks and the foaming sea. They came upon two trees left behind by the falling tide, one of ash and one of elm. From the ash the gods shaped a man and from the elm they carved a woman. Odin breathed into them spirit, Vili provided them with reason and motion, and Ve endowed them with speech and the senses. The man they called Ask and the woman Embla. They were given the place of Midgard to live in, and over the years the land was peopled with their children and their children's children. Other gods came to join Odin, Vili and Ve. At the centre of the universe together the gods made for themselves their splendid abode, Asgard, within which was Hlidskialf, the lofty throne of Odin. From his high seat he could look out over the whole world, observing the works of all men, contemplating all that he saw.

Night, the dark-eyed, dark-skinned daughter of the giant Niorvi, married a man called Naglfari, and by him had a son called Aud. Later she married a second time to a man called Annar, and their daughter was called Jord (earth). Her third marriage was to the god Delling of the race of Aesir, their son, a child of beauty and brightness, was called Dagr (day). Then Odin took Night and her son Dagr and gave them horses and chariots to drive across the heavens one after the other, each taking 12 hours to circle the world. First rides Night in her chariot drawn by her horse Hrimfaxi, from whose foaming mouth falls the dew each morning as he ends his journey. Then comes Dagr drawn by his horse Skinfaxi, from whose mane light falls over the earth and sky.

There was a man of Midgard, called Mundilfari, who had two children who were so fair and graceful that he named them Mani (moon) and Sol (sun), after the two heavenly spheres. The gods were so enraged at his presumption that they took them and placed them in the sky, bidding them to drive the chariots of the sun and moon. Sol drove the chariot of the sun, and her brother Mani that of the moon, governing waxing and waning as he went. One day Mani saw two children named Hjuki and Bil (the Jack and Jill of the nursery rhyme) as they were returning from the spring of Byrgir, carrying a bucket between them. As he passed he reached down and carried them off. Their father, Vidfinn, follows the moon tirelessly in the hope of rescuing his beloved children.

The sun rushes across the sky at speed chased by the snarling wolf, Skoll. She fears that he will one day catch and devour her. A second wolf, Hati, runs before her, chasing the moon with similar intent. These wolves are the fell sons of an old hag living to the east of Midgard in Jarnvid the Iron Wood, the land of the witches who are known as the Jarnvidjur.

Beneath the earth, maggots grew from the flesh of Ymir. By the will of the gods they took the semblance and wits of men, but they were smaller in stature, and dark skinned. The gods called them dwarfs. Their leaders were Modsognir and Durin. They live forever under the hills, beneath the mountains, in their earthen homes and rocky caverns, shunning the lighted world of man.

So Midgard lies, fashioned by the art and will of the sons of Bor. Beneath the open sky, the sea laps upon its sandy and rock-strewn shore and the green grass sways quietly in the gentle breeze.

odin

Odin, known also as Wotan or Woden, was the leader of the Viking gods. He was a sky god and god of wisdom, he was the god of war and death. As many of the gods were descended from him he was called Allfather.

With his spear of ash Gungnir and his marvellous ring Draupnir he ruled Asgard, the realm of the gods. The spear was especially associated with his worship, men dying a bloodless death would ask to be marked with a spear so that they might enter Asgard rather than go to the kingdom of Hel. Also, before a battle, a spear would be thrown over the opposing army and an oath made promising Odin the enemy dead as a gift in exchange for providing victory.

His ravens Hugin (thought) and Munin (memory) perched by him as he sat upon his throne Hlidskialf. These birds would fly out each dawn and return at dusk carrying news of all that they had seen or heard. At his feet lay two wolves, Geri and Freki. The raven and the wolf were beast of the battlefield and so were sacred to Odin.

Odin had a hall called Valhalla (hall of the slain), which had 540 doors, walls made of brightly polished spears and a roof of golden shields. It was here that he greeted warriors fallen in battle. They became part of his battle host, the Einheriar, who would spend each day fighting, re-enacting the martial feats of their mortal life. As night fell all their injuries and wounds would be completely healed and they would spend the dark hours feasting at Odin's rich and plentiful table, carefully attended by the Valkyrs, the warrior maidens of Odin. In Valhalla the warriors drank great quantities of mead, which was provided by the goat Heidrun, who lived amongst the topmost branches of Yggdrasil, the World Tree. For meat they were supplied with the flesh of the boar Saehrimnir, which was killed each day by the cook Andhrimnir and prepared in the cauldron Eldhrimnir.

the origin of poetry

For many long and weary years a war had been waged between the two rival groups of gods, the Aesir of Asgard and the Vanir of Vanaheim. Tiring of battle, the two sides met to settle the dispute peaceably. Their agreement was confirmed by each of them spitting into a ceremonial jar. As a symbol of their peace they took the contents of the jar and formed a being who they named Kvasir. They bestowed upon him such a degree of intelligence that he was able to answer any question that was asked of him.

Kvasir left the gods and travelled the whole of the earth teaching men wisdom. Two dwarfs named Fjalar and Galar were envious of his wide knowledge and treacherously they murdered him. By adding honey to his blood, they brewed a mead of such potent quality that whoever drank but the smallest sip would receive the gift of poetry and song. The gods, perceiving that Kvasir had come to grief, sought out the dwarfs and questioned them deeply. But they answered

that he had died of an excess of his own wisdom, as he could not find anyone to test his abilities to their full, he had lost the will to live.

A little time later the two dwarfs needlessly drowned a giant named Gilling and murdered his wife. The giant's son Suttung sought to avenge the death of his parents by stranding the dwarfs upon a lonely rock far out to sea which he knew would be covered by the incoming tide. As he was leaving them to their fate they implored him to spare them and offered the liquid of inspiration as payment of wergeld, (the price of compensation due to the family of murder victims). Suttung took the potion and left the dwarfs in the hands of his daughter Gunnlauth. As a result poetry was known amongst the Northern skalds by the names of Kvasir's Blood, Suttung's Mead and the Dwarfs' Ransom.

When Odin heard of the mead, he was determined to possess it for himself. In disguise and calling himself by the name Baulverk, he set out for Jotunheim, and after many days of travelling came to the fields of Suttung's brother, Baugi. There he found nine thralls mowing, and he spoke to them offering to sharpen their scythes with his whetstone. They were grateful for his help and when he was done they found their blades so sharp that they asked if he would be willing to part with it. In answer Odin threw it up in the

air. The thralls all rushed to catch it, but in doing so, each ran upon the scythe of one of his fellows, so that they were all killed in their haste.

Odin left the dead thralls and later in the day found himself at the hall of Baugi. The giant told him of his sad loss, his nine men had killed each other and he was without labour. Odin said that for a draught of Suttung's mead, he would himself do the work of the thralls. Baugi agreed and so Odin worked for the whole summer doing the work of nine men.

When the time came for him to receive his payment, Baugi could not persuade his brother to part with any of the precious mead. So together Odin and the giant sought a way to steal it. They discovered that Suttung's daughter held it for her father in safe keeping at her cave. Baugi bored a hole into the cave and Odin, in the form of a worm, crawled through a gap. Once inside the cave he resumed his normal stature and won the heart of the giant's daughter.

After spending three days and three nights with the giantess Odin had no trouble in persuading her to let him drink from each of the three cups (whose names were Odhroerir, Bodn and Son) in which the mead was held. Taking advantage of his good fortune he drank so deeply that all the jars were emptied. Then, assuming the shape of an eagle, he flew off towards Asgard as fast as he was able, but Suttung, who had discovered his purpose, also took that shape and followed after him. As Odin neared Asgard, the Aesir saw him coming. Knowing of his errand they gathered together all the jars they could lay their hands upon and set them out in the fields. No sooner had they done this than Odin, flying above, spewed out the magical mead. He was so close to being caught by Suttung that not all the mead fell into the jars of the gods; some were lost. However, that mead which was caught was reserved for the use of the gods and those men having the knowledge to make proper use of it. So poetry is also known as Odin's Booty, Odin's Gift and the Mead of the Gods.

the Birth of sleipnir

Before the gods had completed their home of Asgard, but after they had finished Midgard and Valhalla, there came to them a man who was a skilled builder. He offered to build for them, in three and a half years, a stronghold so secure that even if the frost giants and the mountain giants managed to penetrate into Midgard, the gods would still be safe. For payment however he demanded the beautiful goddess Freya, and also the sun and the moon.

The gods devoted a great length of time to considering his proposals. Eventually they agreed, but only on the condition that he would complete the whole of the work, without any assistance in the space of one winter, and further, if any part of the work should remain uncompleted on the first day of summer, he would not receive any of his payment. On hearing these terms the man asked if he might be allowed the use of his horse, Svadilfari, and upon the advice of Loki the gods agreed to his request.

The work was begun on the first day of winter. Throughout each day the man worked, building the walls with great skill, and throughout each night the horse would bring stone. The size of the stones amazed the gods, so large were they. They soon realized that the horse did twice the work of the man. However they had made their bargain, and sworn solemn oaths, so they could do nothing but wait and watch as the walls grew higher.

Through the cold winter snows and the chilling blasts of the north wind, the man and his horse worked on, night and day. Frost and ice swept all around them as they toiled, the crystal splinters clinging to their hair and biting into their pale numbed flesh.

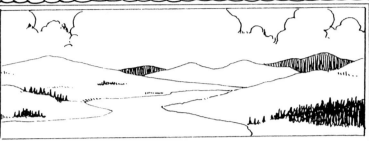

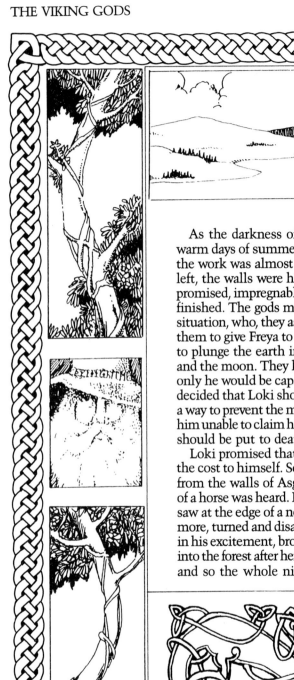

As the darkness of winter drew behind them and the warm days of summer approached the gods perceived that the work was almost complete. With three days of winter left, the walls were high, broad and long and, as had been promised, impregnable. Only the gatehouse remained to be finished. The gods met in the hall of justice to review the situation, who, they asked one another, who had counselled them to give Freya to the man, and who had advised them to plunge the earth into darkness by giving away the sun and the moon. They knew only Loki could be responsible, only he would be capable of such unsound wisdom. It was decided that Loki should find a solution to their difficulty, a way to prevent the man completing his work and so render him unable to claim his expected reward. If not then he, Loki, should be put to death for his crime.

Loki promised that he would do their bidding whatever the cost to himself. So that night, as the man led Svadilfari from the walls of Asgard to collect more stone, the neigh of a horse was heard. Looking around in the dim light, they saw at the edge of a nearby forest a mare. She neighed once more, turned and disappeared amongst the trees. Svadilfari, in his excitement, broke away from his master and galloped into the forest after her. The man had no choice but to follow, and so the whole night was lost, the man searching for

Svadilfari, and Svadilfari searching for the mare. By day-break the work had not progressed from the evening before. Seeing this, and in order to make up for the lost time, the man cast off his disguise and began to grow. On reaching his true size the gods saw that he was in reality a mountain giant.

Regarding their oaths and promises no longer valid the gods called upon Thor to avenge them. He came quickly to their assistance and with one deftly aimed swing of his hammer he shattered the giant's skull and hurled him bodily into Niflheim. However, during the night, Loki had been found by Svadilfari still in the shape of a mare and shortly afterwards bore a strange grey foal with eight legs. This horse the gods named Sleipnir.

frigga, queen of the gods

F rigga was the tall, beautiful daughter of Fiorgyn; she was the sister of Jord and, as wife of Odin, was known as the mother of the gods. As the goddess of the sky she wore softly draping garments of purest white, reflecting the colour of the bright clouds. At other times she would be robed in the deeper shades of storms and midnight hues.

When she married Odin there was a great feast of rejoicing, for the Aesir loved her dearly. Indeed it became their custom to celebrate the occasion annually with a festival of joy and happiness. She had strong links with marriage and fertility, and a toast to her health was always proposed at wedding feasts, along with that of Odin and Thor. Sometimes alone, sometimes with Odin, she would sit upon the throne Hlidskialf, and look out over the world. She had the power to see the future, but would reveal her sacred knowledge to no one.

She lived in the welcoming hall of Fensalir, where the husbands and wives who had been faithful to one another on earth would be reunited after death, never to be separated again. It was here too that she would work at her spinning-wheel, spinning out long threads of golden cloud. The stars we know as Orion's Belt were called by the Northern peoples Frigga's Spinning-Wheel.

Frigga had several goddesses as attendants of who the best known were Fulla, Hlin and Gna. Fulla, who was according to some her sister, was most often at Frigga's side advising her and sharing her confidence. She was beautiful and wore a fine gold band around her long golden hair which hung loose about her shoulders. Hlin acted as an intermediary between Frigga and her followers, carrying news of their prayers to her mistress. It was also her duty to attend to those in times of trouble or grief, offering them comfort, reassurance and hope. Gna was Frigga's trusted messenger who, mounted upon the horse Hofvarpnir (hoof thrower), would cut swiftly through the air like the refreshing breeze.

41

Another was Lofn (love), who saw that nothing hindered lovers in their search for happiness. Vjofn had the task of calming quarrels between man and wife, and spreading peace among the people of Midgard.

Guarding the doors of Frigga's hall was Syn (truth), who would obstruct and bar the way against those who were not allowed to enter. Her decision was final — once someone had been turned away nothing could induce her to change her mind. She had therefore an interest in judicial trials and if an idea or suggestion was rejected then it was said that Syn must be against it.

The goddess of medicine and healing was also one of her attendants. Her name was Eira and she would scour the whole earth for powerful ingredients and rare herbs for her remedies. She taught her skills with care to the women of the Northern peoples who, following her fine example, became accomplished healers. Vara punished those who deliberately lied under oath or failed to keep their word. The goddess of virtue was Snotra, who had achieved knowledge of a great many things. Vor (faith) had full vision of the future, seeing clearly all that was about to happen upon the world of men.

fRigga and the golden Ring

F rigga had such an overwhelming love for sparkling jewellery and colourful ornament, that it once led to her downfall.

Looking from the heights of Hlidskialf, into the temple of Odin, she saw that there was an offering of gold before his statue. Again and again as she watched over the actions of man, her eye was drawn back to the temple. The more she looked at the gold the more her heart longed for its possession. It consumed her mind so much that she could think of nothing else. Eventually, with her movements hidden in the darkness of night, she crept forth. Her fingers trembled with desire as she tightly grasped the gold. It was hers, she had stolen the offering to Odin. The mother of the gods carried her prize to the dwarf smiths who, with their dark cunning, fashioned the gold into a glorious necklace. The jewel was so well made that when she wore it around her slender neck Odin's love for her redoubled.

After a time the theft of the gold became known to him. He summoned the dwarfs and commanded them to name the one who had dared to desecrate the sanctity of his temple and steal his offering. But the dwarfs said nothing. Such was their love for Frigga they refused to betray her.

Odin, realizing that questioning the dark elves was useless, went to his temple and stood before the statue.

Working powerful runes he began his magic, aiming to give the wooden image the gift of speech so that it would provide him with the name of the one he sought.

Frigga was filled with worry when she discovered her husband's intent. Not knowing what to do, she called on her servant Fulla to help save her from his anger. Fulla acted instantly, setting out immediately in search of the one who would be most able to assist her mistress. Soon she returned with a hideous dark elf, who on the promise of a handsome reward swore to defeat Odin's plan.

The dwarf crept stealthily to the door of the temple, where the guards stood keeping watch in the cold chill of the night. With his magic he cast a deep sleep over Odin's watchmen and stepping nimbly over their slumbering bodies he entered. Pressing the whole weight of his small form against the base of the statue he began to rock it back and forth. The carved image above him started to move gently, then it swayed from side to side and at last it rocked dangerously and fell crashing to the ground, shattering all around him. There it lay until morning, when Odin himself discovered its fragmented pieces strewn across the temple floor. Despite all his efforts he failed to give it the power of speech.

Odin was so angered that he gathered all the treasures of the gods and left Asgard to its fate. In his absence his brothers

Vili and Ve usurped his power and took his throne for themselves. But they were unable to keep the frost giants from invading the earth. Indeed the whole of Midgard came under the sway of the fearsome giants and with them they brought a terrible winter. The waters froze and the earth became hardened and unyielding. Snow fell thick and deep, blanketing the land.

After seven long months, Odin finally returned. When he saw the evil over the realm, he searched for his brothers and banished them from Asgard. He then sought out the frost giants, commanded them to relinquish their icy grasp on the land and drove to the boundaries of the earthly kingdom. The earth slowly warmed and rejoiced at his home-coming, and young shoots of green vegetation sprang up to welcome him. The rivers ran again released from their frozen bonds, while in the fields men worked hard and long hours with ploughs and oxen, happy with the promise of a good harvest.

odin outwitted

As darkness approached the rain began to fall heavily. There had been a steady drizzle all through the afternoon but now the grey skies opened and the cold rain poured down upon the muddy heath. Through the failing light camp-fires burned brightly on either side of the wide valley. Around the fires huddled figures were stationed. One by one they moved, shuffling closer to the reassuring glow and pulling their thick cloaks tightly about their heads.

The two armies prepared themselves for the night. The Winilars camped to the North and the Vandals to the South. They were sworn enemies, both waiting for the dawn. Each man, hunched uncomfortably in wet clothing, thought silently of the battle that the morning would bring. There was no warmth in the fires, no warmth in their bodies. The chilling downpour cut to their very souls, invading their minds with dank despair.

A solitary voice began to chant; soon it was joined by many others. Then a second song arose opposing the first. In different tongues, the two songs gave new hope; growing and

expanding it surged around the camps. Fear and worries were cast into the shadows behind them as confidence and assurety gained a firm hold of their hearts. With water dripping down from their brows they sang out. Their pale rain-streaked faces shone red, reflecting the light of the hissing flames. Deep strong voices raised up to heaven, calling out to their gods for victory. The Winilers appealed to the goddess Frigga for aid, while the Vandals invoked Odin the god of war to bring them glory.

Far away in Asgard, high upon the throne of Hlidskialf, Odin and Frigga looked down upon the scene watching with interest. Frigga turned to her husband and asked casually who he would favour with victory. He privately supported the Vandals; however, not wishing to displease her, he avoided answering the question saying that it was now night and time for rest, adding that the victors would be whichever army his eye fell upon first when he awoke the next day.

Frigga saw through his trick, she knew that from where he lay upon his bed he would look out upon the Vandals. She waited until he was deep in slumber and carefully turned his bed around until it faced her favourites. Then she sent a message to the Winilers, bidding them to dress their women for battle in the morning, with their hair carefully combed down to cover their cheeks and breasts. By the fading

light of their smouldering fires they resolved to do as she had said.

Through the chilling drizzle, the grey light of dawn spread slowly from the East. Faint and uncertain at first, the outlines of warriors gradually took shape with the coming of day — grim faces and hard eyes. Two armies stood in the sodden grass, their cold fingers tightening wet leather sword-belts, chilled hands grasping cruel iron-tipped spears. In silence they prepared themselves for battle.

'What Longbeards are these?' asked Odin as he woke, failing to recognize the assembled host. Frigga saw immediately that her plan had been successful. Not only had he first looked out upon her followers, but he had also given them a new name, which as ancient custom required should be accompanied by a baptismal gift. The goddess demanded that Odin's gift should be the outright victory which she desired for them. Seeing how cleverly he had been outwitted he made no complaint and gave them victory over the Vandals. In memory of Odin's support that day, the Winilers chose to be known by their newly given name for ever afterwards — the name which came eventually to be Lombards. Pleased at their recognition of his help the father of the gods watched over them with special care from that time onwards.

Balder the Bright

The most loved of all the Aesir was Balder, the beautiful son of Odin and Frigga. As his brother Hodur was the god of darkness, so he was the god of radiance and light. His hair fell about his innocent face like beams of golden sunlight. His very appearance brought gladness to the hearts of all who saw him. He had a great knowledge of magic and was well practised in the lore of runes, which Odin had engraved upon his tongue. His loving wife was Nanna (blossom), she was the beautiful daughter of Nip (bud). Together they lived in the hall of Breidablik, roofed with fine silver and walled with burnished gold. The place was so sacred that nothing unclean was ever allowed to enter within its glittering walls.

hermod

As the messenger of the gods, Hermod was ready to leave Asgard at a moment's notice. With no thoughts of danger or discomfort, he was prepared to carry out any errand that might be required of him. In thanks for this trustworthy service, his father Odin presented him with a fine warrior's helmet and a coat of strong mail. He also possessed a staff called Gambanein which he carried wherever he went. Occasionally he would take Odin's spear Gungnir and joyfully ride in battle with the Valkyrs.

the wizard of the north

Far to the North, where the winds are cold and the land is forever frozen, there lived the people called the Finns. They were an ancient race even then, rich in the knowledge of secret things.

One of them was Rossthiof (horse thief), whose fame spread far and wide. He was known for his many powers, of which his ability to divine the future far surpassed all others. However he was a selfish creature and put his magical powers to evil use. He made a considerable profit from his black art, amassing a vast fortune of precious gold and sparkling jewels. In his hall, surrounded by the swirling and drifting snow, he would prepare his magic. He sent invisible fingers reaching out through the cold air and entering deep into the innocent minds of travellers. His sorcery tugged and pulled at them, drawing them, irresistably calling them to come to his brightly lit and appealing hall. Once he had them within his walls, they had little hope of continuing their journey, for his sole desire was to kill them and keep their valuable possessions for himself.

Odin, concerned about the uncertainty of the future and unable to obtain satisfaction from the all-knowing Norns thought to consult the northern wizard. Asking Hermod to go and question Rossthiof, Odin lent him his horse Sleipnir and also his own personal rune staff, which would counter the magician's evil magic.

The wizard invoked dark conjurations, phantasms and illusions against the approaching Hermod. Great dragons of ice and flame rose up before him and giants wielding iron-spiked clubs barred his path. Wolves with burning eyes gathered around him, baring their teeth as they snarled and howled. But at the sight of the rune staff they all cowered back. First the dragons melted, returning to the snow from which they were formed, then the giants lost their solidity and faded into the evening mist, and finally the wolves ceased their clamour and skulked off into the night. Before the power of the staff all the wizard's efforts to ensnare him came to nought and Hermod was able to reach his cold northern home unscathed. Striding boldly into his hall the god was easily able to subdue the Finn. He bound him with a strong rope, and threatened never to release him unless he promised to reveal the future.

Now afraid of the god's strong magic, the captive Rossthiof agreed, and was duly set free from his bonds to do his work. Muttering dark unearthly words, vibrating long low syllables, his voice seemed almost inhuman as he worked his age-old magic.

High above, the sun hid her face in horror, such was the strength of the gathering power. The earth moved and groaned underfoot, and on all sides the wind shrieked like tormented demons. Suddenly the wizard raised his hand and pointed to the horizon. 'Look!' he cried, above the sound of the raging storm, 'Look!' A gap had appeared high within the dark storming clouds and a great shaft of burning light burst through. Below, the ground became the deepest red. A liquid flow, the rich colour of newly-spilled blood. A beautiful woman appeared above the ruddy stream, then beside her there was a child, her son. The child grew, so quickly he grew, soon he was his full manly height. Beside his mother he stood, his strong hands holding a strong bow and many sharp iron-tipped arrows.

When the vision had faded, and the storm had blown its final icy blast, the wizard turned to the astonished Hermod. He then explained the meaning of all that they had witnessed in that hour. The stream of blood, he said, foretold

the murder of one of Odin's sons. But if the Allfather sought out the beautiful princess Rinda, he would have by her a son. The child would develop quickly and within a few hours attain his full height. Then he would be ready to step forth and avenge his brother's death.

Returning to Asgard, Hermod conveyed to Odin the full content of the Rossthiof's message. Odin, finding his fears confirmed by Hermod's words, was able to seek some consolation in the thought that although he might lose one son to a violent end, a second and as yet unborn son would redress the crime.

55

TYR

yr was once the supreme sky god of the Northern peoples, but as time progressed his position and some of his attributes were usurped by the god Odin. Eventually Tyr became one of Odin's sons, his mother being either Frigga or an unknown but beautiful giantess. Although he became overshadowed by Odin, he was still considered to be one of the 12 principal gods of Asgard, and sat on one of the 12 thrones in Gladsheim, the hall of judgement. He stood beside Odin as god of war — often the two were invoked together by those wishing for success in battle.

His prized possession was his sword, and sword-dances were performed in his honour. Oaths were sworn upon the blades of swords in his name. His rune was carved or scratched upon warriors' swords to bring them luck in battle.

the Binding of Fenris

oki lived for a time in secret with the hideous giantess, Angurboda (anguish boding), amid the rocky hillsides of Jotunheim. There she bore him three children of monstrous aspect. These ill-made offspring were Fenris the savage wolf, Hel the goddess of death, and Iormungandr the terrible World Serpent.

For many years they kept the existence of their progeny from the gods in Asgard. But they grew to such a size that they could no longer stay hidden in the cave of their birth. One morning Odin looked from his throne Hlidskialf, and chanced to see them. From then on he watched them daily. Alarmed at their rapid rate of growth he resolved to get rid of them before they became a danger to the gods.

Hel he cast down into the darkest depths of the earth, to rule over Niflheim the dismal land of the dead. Iormungandr he threw into the sea, where benefitting from his new environment he grew and grew until he circled the earth. Odin chose to keep Fenris, thinking that if he might be tamed, he would guard the walls of Asgard from their enemies and serve the gods well. The gods though were ill at ease with the beast, and only the brave Tyr dared to approach him. But the wolf grew larger and as he grew he became even more ferocious than before. Seeing this the Aesir assembled to decide what might be done with him. They thought it would be wrong to kill the beast when they had brought the problem upon themselves, so they agreed to bind him so tightly that he could do no harm.

They tricked the unsuspecting Fenris into being tied with a chain of strong iron links called Laeding. But his strength was such that he burst his bonds with ease and cast the broken chain to the ground. Heartily praising the wolf's great strength the worried gods went off and obtained a second chain, Droma, many times stronger than the first, but Fenris, with a fearsome display of strength, burst this one too.

Finally the Aesir, seeing that no common binding would hold the mighty wolf, sent Skirnir, Frey's servant, down to Svartalfheim to procure from the dwarfs an unbreakable bond. With the aid of magic the dwarfs created Gleipnir, a wonderful rope made from the sound of a cat's footsteps, a woman's beard and the roots of mountains. Giving it to Skirnir, they assured him that nothing would cause it to fail, because as more force was applied, the stronger it would become.

Fenris, who by now had grown even stronger, did not trust the gods and their games of strength, and refused to allow any further tests to be made unless one of their number would be willing to place his arm between the wolf's powerful jaws as a guarantee against treachery.

Seeing that no other god would come forward, Tyr placed his hand bravely between the wolf's glistening teeth. Quickly the gods bound Fenris with the magical rope. When they saw that he was unable to break free they were overjoyed. All but Tyr, for the wolf, discovering the strength of his bonds, had bitten off the god's hand at the wrist.

The gods then tied the rope to the rock Thviti which they sank deep beneath the ground. There he would stay until the end of time when he would break free and meet the Aesir once more in their final hour.

Loki

Loki's character was complex — at times he was merely the originator of childlike mischief, whilst at others he was capable of the most evil treachery. He had the ability and the quick wits to extricate the gods from some particularly embarrassing situations; however he was usually responsible for getting them into these same situations. Despite this, in many of the myths the gods were happy to have him accompany them on their adventures, and on these occasions he showed nothing of his mischievous nature. Loki was not only the father of the three terrible monsters, Fenris, Iormungandr and Hel, but he himself also gave birth to the horse Sleipnir.

Eventually he brought about the final downfall of the gods. First he was responsible for Balder's death, and secondly, in the guise of Thaukt, Loki was the only one in the whole of the nine worlds not to weep for him, Balder then being in the power of Hel, Loki's daughter. Later at the final battle he and his three monstrous children fight on the side of the Surt and the frost giants, in opposition to the gods.

Frey

Frey was the son of Niord and brother to Freya. They came with their father from Vanaheim as the hostages of the Aesir. When Frey cut his first tooth the gods of Asgard gave him a gift as was the practice among the Northern peoples. They gave him the wondrous land of Alfheim, the home of the Light Elves. There Frey, the god of vegetation and prosperity, lived happily amongst his faithful subjects the elves.

Later he was presented with a wondrous sword. It had the ability to fight magically, as soon as it was released from its scabbard, without the need of a guiding hand. Frey put this weapon to good effect against the hated frost giants. From the dwarfs of Svartalfheim he received the marvellous golden boar, Gullinbursti (golden bristled), who pulled him in his chariot. At other times he would ride upon his fearless horse, Blodughofi, who was ready to face any peril at his master's command.

Frey's most valuable possession was his ship, the fabulous Skidbladnir, again made by the dwarfs. Aboard this vessel Frey could travel over land and sea, always sure of a favourable wind. It had the property of being so artfully designed that it was large enough to carry all the gods and their horses — and have room for more. It could also be folded up like fine parchment to fit in the small bag on his belt.

frey and gerda

One day Frey sat in Odin's seat, the towering Hlidskialf and looked out over the whole world. Eventually his eye fell upon a well-proportioned northern hall. There was a woman walking up towards the door, and as she raised her hand to push the door aside he caught sight of her face. He was astonished by her great beauty. The hall belonged to a man called Gymir, the husband of Aurboda a mountain giant. The woman that Frey saw was their daughter Gerda.

Frey climbed down from the high seat of Odin, his mind filled with sorrow. When he returned to the company of the other gods he would neither speak nor eat and such was the expression of his face that none dared to ask what troubled him. At last the gods could suffer the sight of the afflicted Frey no longer. Niord called for Skirnir, his son's servant, and commanded him to discover the source of Frey's sadness. Fearful of bringing his master's anger down upon himself, Skirnir tactfully questioned the silent Frey. Frey however answered gladly, telling his servant of the woman he had seen and how he longed to be with her, so much indeed that he feared he should not live without her.

Deciding on action he sent Skirnir to Gerda, to ask her hand in marriage and bring her to Asgard whether her father consented or not. Frey even made him a gift of his magical sword for protection in the land of the giants, so anxious was he that his errand should succeed. As Skirnir took his leave of the god, he bent and filled his drinking horn from the nearby stream, catching along with the water Frey's reflection.

Riding Frey's horse Blodughofi, with 11 golden apples and the magical ring Draupnir in his bag, he arrived in Jotunheim. The sound of barking dogs met him as he approached Gymir's hall. Then as he came closer he saw a gigantic wall of raging flame before him, but the brave Blodughofi galloped on through the burning heat to the giant's door.

When he came before the fair Gerda, Skirnir revealed to her the reflected face of Frey, delivered his message of love, and offered her the apples and the wonderful ring. But she refused his proposal and would accept none of the gifts. Her father, she said, had more than enough gold and valuable treasures to spare.

Annoyed at her rejection of his master, Skirnir threatened to cut off her head with his sword if she did not consent to marriage, but she stood firm before him, defiant and unafraid. Finally, when all else had failed, he resorted to magic. Taking his knife, he began to cut powerful runes upon his staff. He warned her that if she did not agree to Frey's wishes before he came to the end of his spell, she would be bound to remain unmarried for ever or else wed some evil frost giant for whom she could find no love. She was appalled at the prospect of such a frightful future, so reluctantly she declared that she would become the god's wife and arranged to meet him at a place called Buri when nine nights had passed.

Frey was overjoyed to hear of Gerda's acceptance, but on learning that he would have to pass nine long nights without her he became sad once more. Eventually though his waiting was over, and as darkness fell at the end of the eighth day he rushed to the meeting place and found Gerda his bride waiting for him. She became his loving wife and ruled Alfheim beside him.

In another story Gerda's brother, Beli, attacked her husband and Frey, having no sword to defend himself, tore a stag's horn from the wall of his house and used it as a weapon. Despite his disadvantaged position and his great reluctance to shed the blood of his wife's kin, his foe soon lay dead at his feet. Gerda's grief however was soon forgotten when she gave birth to Frey's child, Fiolnir.

freya

Freya was the goddess of love and beauty. She was born in Vanaheim, and was the twin sister of Frey. She was considered by some to be the goddess Frigga under another name, but others saw her as an entirely separate deity. As one of the Vanir, and like Frigga, she was also a goddess of the earth and fertility.

The beautiful blue-eyed, golden-haired Freya would always listen to the prayers of lovers, and help them whenever she could. But she had other duties besides being the goddess of love. It was she who led the Valkyrs (choosers of the slain). She would lead them down from Valhalla to the blood-soaked battlefields below. Among the clashing shields and ringing swords they would weave their way, deciding upon who should fall and who should live. Half of the fallen heroes would go to Valhalla, and the remainder she would escort to her hall Folkvang, where they were met by their faithful wives and loved ones.

The tales of her hall were so inviting and so welcoming that some Northern women sought to accompany their men folk in death as in life. They were known to follow their husbands into battle. If a man was killed on the battlefield, then his wife too would hope to perish there. Failing this they might throw themselves upon their own swords or lie down across the burning funeral pyres of their husbands.

freya and odur

Freya married Odur and had two daughters, Hnoss and Gersemi. She was most happy to be married to her husband and led a contented life in her hall of Folkvang. One day, however, Odur went away, and she knew not where to find him. She wept in sadness, tears falling from her sorrowful eyes and splashing upon the rocks of the earth. The hard rocks became soft and allowed the warm tears to reach their very centres and there they solidified to become fine pieces of the purest gold. Other tears fell into the sea and became amber of the most beautiful quality.

The weeks passed but he did not return. Eventually the day came when she could no longer bear to be without her beloved husband. So, mounting her chariot which was drawn by two cats, she left her lonely hall, and bidding farewell to the Aesir passed out of Asgard. She travelled over many lands, asking all she met for news of Odur. But no one had seen him pass by, no one had heard of his whereabouts. So on and on, shedding many tears as she journeyed through the nine worlds. As a result of her weeping gold may be found in all the lands of the earth.

Finally with the sun high in the Northern sky she found him. He was sitting silently under a myrtle tree, his mind on distant things. His face brightened when he saw her and without offering any word of explanation he gladly agreed to accompany her back to Asgard. As they travelled happily homewards together all of nature rejoiced at their smiling faces.

BRÍSÍNGAMEN

Freya was travelling in Svartalfheim one day when she came across four dwarfs. Their names were Alfrigg, Berling, Dvalin and Grerr, and they were working hard in the heat of their underground workshop. Between them they were fashioning the most wonderful necklace the goddess had ever seen. Its name was Brisingamen.

Immediately she fell in love with it, and begged the dwarfs to give it to her. The dwarfs however refused unless Freya would grant each of them a favour. They had little need of payment in gold or silver, they said; all they asked was that she would spend a night with each of them. She had to possess the necklace so she did as they requested, and after four nights Brisingamen adorned her beautiful neck.

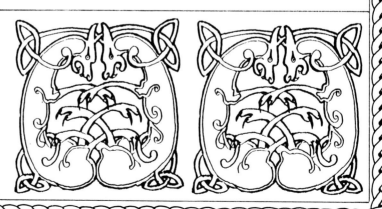

niord, god of the sea

N iord was the father of Frey and Freya. He lived in a part of Asgard near the sea, a place called Noatun. He was the god of summer and the sea, and would grant good winds and weather to those farmers and fishermen who pleased him. He gave storms to those who did not. Niord came originally to Asgard as a hostage from the Vanir, to ensure that their peace with the Aesir was never violated. His first wife was Nerthus, Mother Earth, but she remained behind when he moved to Asgard.

Niord later married Skadi, the personification of winter. However the couple were ill-suited. She was the daughter of the giant, Thjassi, and she preferred to live in her family home among the wild mountains of Thrymheim, whereas Niord longed for his beloved sea. A compromise was eventually made. They would spend nine nights in Thrymheim followed by three in Noatun.

But after his first nine nights away from the sea Niord vowed never to leave it again, preferring the mew of the gulls and the cry of the seal to the chilling howl of the wolf. Likewise, Skadi found the noise of these birds anything but pleasant and hated everything associated with the sea, so she left Niord to spend her days hunting amongst the cold, snow-capped peaks of her homeland. Eventually she married again and lived in happiness with Ullr the god of winter.

aegir

egir was a god of the oceans, he spent his time either in his kingdom beneath the waves, or upon the island of Lessoe. His brothers were Kari (air) and Loki (fire), together they came from an older group of gods than both the Aesir and the Vanir. He married his sister who was Ran (robber), and together the two deities of the sea had nine daughters. These were the beautiful Wave Maidens who, clad in blue or green, would play about the prows of ships, dancing in the water before them or singing with their brother the wind.

Rising up from the depths of the sea, Aegir's long white beard would swirl amidst the churning waters. He would reach out with grasping hands at helpless ships, rolling them over and dragging them down into the deep. Aegir's wife, Ran, was often to be found lurking near dangerous hidden rocks, waiting for unwary mariners. She had a net of tremendous size in which she caught luckless vessels and pulled them against the wood-splintering stones. She was considered by the Northern peoples to preside over those who died at sea, welcoming them to her gold-lined hall. Indeed gold had a special significance in the minds of sailors. Whenever danger threatened at sea, it was customary to hide a small piece of the precious metal about their persons, and so win her good favour.

Aegir had many names among the people of the Northern lands. To the Anglo-Saxons he was known as Eagor, to others his name was Hler (shelterer) or Gymir (concealer). When the waters of the sea stormed and churned it was known as Aegir's Cauldron.

Bragi

O din went to great lengths to win the mead of poetry; however he seldom used it, choosing instead to reserve the potent mixture for his son, Bragi. So Bragi became the god of poetry and of poets. With his white beard and golden harp, his eloquent voice would enrich the feasts of the Aesir with marvellous words, describing skilfully the famous deeds of gods and heroes.

Bragi's Birth

W hen Gunlod bore Bragi her son, deep within her lofty cave, dwarfs came and bestowed upon him the wonderful gift of a magical harp. They took the child and laying him in a ship of their own making sent him out into the world. The boat floated out, driven by the underground river, from his mother's subterranean halls and passed into the land of Nain, the kingdom of the dwarf of death. The infant Bragi sat up and with the magical harp sang a song that moved heaven, earth and the lands below. All the nine worlds were filled with his sweet song.

The ship sailed on and reaching the sunlit shore the child continued further on foot. Walking along lonely forest paths, through silent valleys and over still moorlands, his clear voice brought music to the land. The trees, rejoicing at his song, sent forth their leafy branches, the grass shone, bejewelled with gleaming flowers, and the heather upon the hills became a purple sea stretching as far as the eye could see.

It was within that forest that he met the fair Idun, the child of Ivald, who was visiting the earth at that time. Together they went to Asgard and were greeted with warmth by the gods. Odin, Bragi's father, led him to one side and after making runes upon his tongue declared him the bard to the Aesir, and bade him sing to the glory of gods and men.

thoR

Thor was the tall, muscular, red-bearded god of thunder. After Odin, his father, he was considered to be the mightiest of all the gods of Asgard.

Even as a child Thor made a great impression upon the gods because of his unusual size and enormous strength. One day Thor's mother, Frigga, found her child playing happily, lifting and tossing into the air 10 huge bails of bearskins. At first she was alarmed, thinking that he might come to some harm, but she soon saw that it was just a child's game to him.

He was usually a happy and good-tempered child, but on occasions he would fly into a violent rage. At these times his mother was unable to keep him under control, so after due consideration it was decided to send him away to live with foster parents. For this formidable task Odin and Frigga delivered their troublesome child into the capable hands of Vingnir (the winged) and Hlora (heat), who soon had him under control, to the great relief of his parents. In grateful recognition for the part they played in his upbringing Thor often went by the names of Vingthor and Hlorrdi.

On achieving the age of manhood, Thor returned into Asgard and was accepted by the gods and honoured with one of the 12 places in the judgement hall. For a home he was given the realm of Trudvang where he built his house,

Bilskinir (lightning). This house had within its lofty walls 540 halls, and was the biggest building ever seen in all of the nine worlds.

Thor was the god of the thralls, the ordinary folk of Midgard. After death their lords and masters would enter Valhalla, but the thralls came to the house of Thor, where they were generously entertained.

While the Aesir were free to ride over Bifrost whenever they wished, Thor would always pass underneath, wading through the rivers Kormt and Ormt and the streams of Kerlaug rather than risk setting the Rainbow Bridge aflame by the tremendous heat of his body.

He had two goats to pull his chariot, their names were Tanngniostir (tooth cracker) and Tanngrisnir (tooth gnasher). Sparks would fly like lightning from their hooves and teeth. As Thor journeyed across the sky the deep rumblings of thunder would be heard from the chariot's rolling iron-rimmed wheels. Thus he was also called Akuthor, meaning Thor the charioteer.

Mjolnir (the crusher) was the name of Thor's magical hammer. However hard and often he threw it, it would come back to him, returning again and again to find his waiting hand. As the hammer was red-hot, he grasped it firmly in an iron gauntlet called Iarngreiper. The third and some say the most remarkable of his wondrous possessions was the magical belt Megingiord, which had the power to double the strength of its wearer. With these magical weapons Thor was able to guard the Aesir and Halls of Asgard and keep them safe from the intrusions of their enemies, the envious giants of Jotunheim.

thor and utgard-loki

One day Thor mounted his chariot with Loki, and together they set out on a journey. They travelled many miles but as time passed by they grew weary and at the approach of nightfall, they begged lodging at a thrall's hut. The thrall, who lived with his son Thialfi and daughter Roska, was happy to have the fine visitors share his humble home, but had little to offer them in the way of food. Seeing this Thor killed his own two goats and after skinning them put them into the cauldron to boil. When the meat was ready Thor and Loki invited the family to join them in supper telling them to throw out the bones undamaged onto the two skins that had been set out beside the fire. But Thialfi took his knife and split one of the thicker bones down its length to get to the marrow.

Early in the twilight of the following morning Thor arose. As the first glorious rays of the sun appeared from over the distant snow-topped mountains he took Miolnir, and lifting it high above him, he consecrated the two goat skins in the name of the sacred hammer. Immediately both goats sprang up, just as alive and whole as they were the evening before, but one of them now had a limp in his hind leg. Observing this Thor was angered and accused the thrall and his children of the deed. Fearing for their lives the family begged his forgiveness and offered all that they owned as compensation. Realizing that they were terrified of him Thor's wrath subsided. He became calm and said that he would spare them their lives if the thrall's two children would become his bondmen and serve him for ever more.

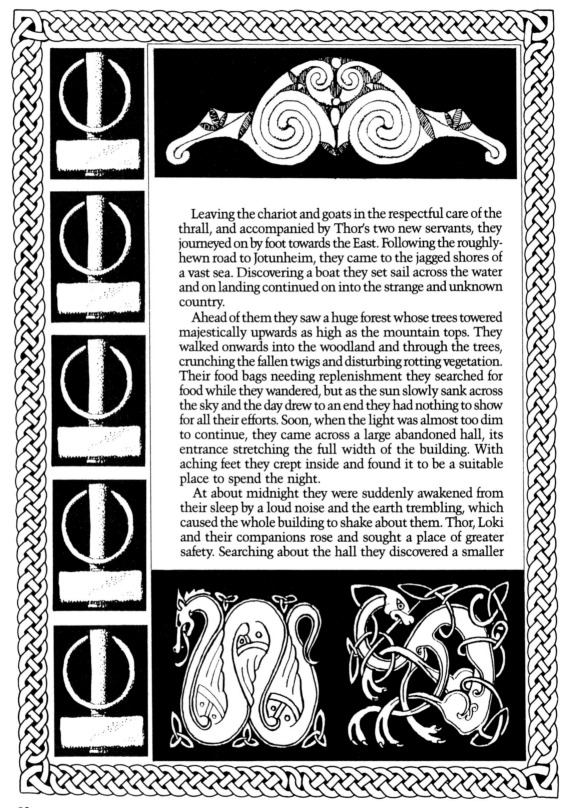

Leaving the chariot and goats in the respectful care of the thrall, and accompanied by Thor's two new servants, they journeyed on by foot towards the East. Following the roughly-hewn road to Jotunheim, they came to the jagged shores of a vast sea. Discovering a boat they set sail across the water and on landing continued on into the strange and unknown country.

Ahead of them they saw a huge forest whose trees towered majestically upwards as high as the mountain tops. They walked onwards into the woodland and through the trees, crunching the fallen twigs and disturbing rotting vegetation. Their food bags needing replenishment they searched for food while they wandered, but as the sun slowly sank across the sky and the day drew to an end they had nothing to show for all their efforts. Soon, when the light was almost too dim to continue, they came across a large abandoned hall, its entrance stretching the full width of the building. With aching feet they crept inside and found it to be a suitable place to spend the night.

At about midnight they were suddenly awakened from their sleep by a loud noise and the earth trembling, which caused the whole building to shake about them. Thor, Loki and their companions rose and sought a place of greater safety. Searching about the hall they discovered a smaller

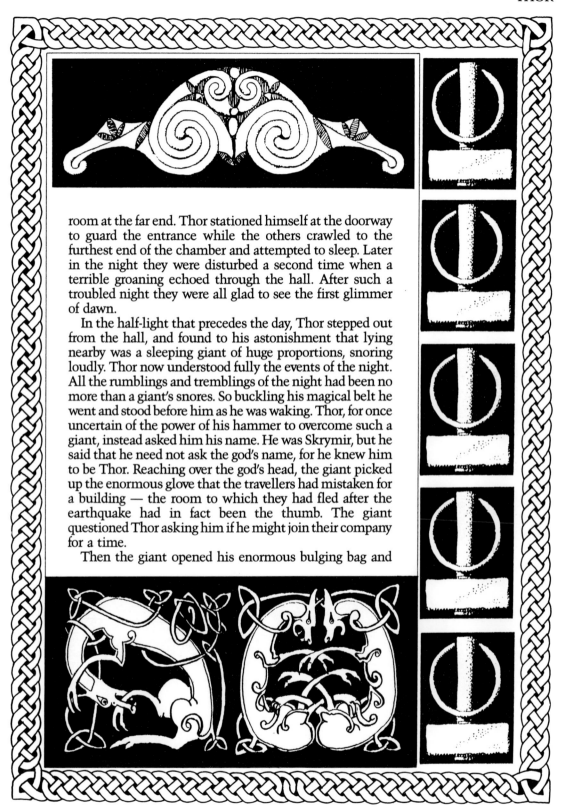

room at the far end. Thor stationed himself at the doorway to guard the entrance while the others crawled to the furthest end of the chamber and attempted to sleep. Later in the night they were disturbed a second time when a terrible groaning echoed through the hall. After such a troubled night they were all glad to see the first glimmer of dawn.

In the half-light that precedes the day, Thor stepped out from the hall, and found to his astonishment that lying nearby was a sleeping giant of huge proportions, snoring loudly. Thor now understood fully the events of the night. All the rumblings and tremblings of the night had been no more than a giant's snores. So buckling his magical belt he went and stood before him as he was waking. Thor, for once uncertain of the power of his hammer to overcome such a giant, instead asked him his name. He was Skrymir, but he said that he need not ask the god's name, for he knew him to be Thor. Reaching over the god's head, the giant picked up the enormous glove that the travellers had mistaken for a building — the room to which they had fled after the earthquake had in fact been the thumb. The giant questioned Thor asking him if he might join their company for a time.

Then the giant opened his enormous bulging bag and

began to eat his breakfast while Thor and the others sat a little way off in the forest. When he had finished Skrymir suggested that they put all their provisions together in one bag, which he slung over his broad shoulder before setting off with long slow giantish strides. At dusk, after walking all day, he found them a place to sleep under a towering oak tree. Then as he lay down to rest he gave them his bag and instructed them to prepare their own supper.

Before long Skrymir was asleep and his deafening snores rang through the wood, but when Thor tried to open the giant's bag he found that he could neither loosen a single knot nor slacken a single string. This so angered Thor that he took his wondrous hammer and smote the resting giant upon the head. Skrymir stirred and asked if a leaf had fallen upon his head, and turning to the god enquired whether they had enjoyed their supper and were they ready to go to sleep. Thor told him that they were just about to make their beds for the night, and stormed off to another tree and lay down.

But Thor stayed awake brooding about the giant. Eventually Skrymir began to snore again, so loudly that the very trees shook and trembled about them. Unable to tolerate this a moment longer Thor rose up and dealt the recumbent giant a second blow much mightier than the first, indeed of such a force that Mjolnir sank into the giant's

skull up to the handle. 'What was that? Did an acorn fall on my head?' called the giant. Thor departed quickly saying that there was still time for sleep before dawn. As he left Skrymir, he vowed that should the occasion arise to permit the striking of a third blow, he should not fail but to slay the giant.

As morning came Skrymir was again in a deep sleep so Thor crept to his side, and with all the strength that he could summon swung his hammer at the giant's skull. Such was the violence of the blow that he forced the hammer into the giant's bristly cheek so far that the handle was all but lost to view. Skrymir sat up and giving his rough cheek a rub said, 'Are there any birds perched in the branches above? I thought that something had fallen on my head!' Then seeing Thor by his side said, 'What, are you awake? Well we should prepare to leave, for you have not far to go now before you reach the city of Utgard'.

He told them that although he was not small himself, there were many who dwelled in Utgard who were much taller than he. Looking at Thor, the champion of the Aesir, he told him that they would not look kindly upon such puny creatures as he, therefore he advised them to turn back. However they insisted on proceeding. Their road lay to the East, while his was to the mountains of the North, so picking

up his bag the giant strode off deep into the forest and was soon lost to sight in the gloom.

The gods and the thralls walked on, picking their route as well as they could over the smashed rocks and the fallen trees that crossed their path. Around noon they emerged from the forest to see before them in the middle of a plain the monstrous city of Utgard. Such was the height of the towers and soaring pinnacles that they had to bend their necks backwards against their shoulders to see the tops. When at last they reached the gatehouse they found the barred iron gate to be firmly locked and bolted against them. However the bars of the gate were of such gigantic dimensions that the travellers gained entrance to the city by squeezing between them.

Once within the walls of Utgard they saw a towering hall before them with its door wide open. They entered and found it to be full of giants of enormous size sitting upon benches that ran down each wall of the long building. At the far end of the hall they observed the king, Utgard-Loki. Boldly they approached him and offered him greetings with the respect due to such a person. Their words were met by a look of scorn from the king who recognized them immediately. He spoke to them nonchalantly, pretending to be surprised at their diminutive stature, asking what prowess they possessed, saying that none was permitted to remain within his hall who did not in some way excel all others.

Loki answered first, it being longer than he wished since his last meal, saying that he could eat faster than anyone present, and was prepared to prove the fact immediately. The king raised an eyebrow. 'That will indeed be a feat,' he remarked with new interest, and ordered one of the giants, whose name was Logi, to come before him and try his skill against Loki. A great wooden trough full of meat was set before them. Loki positioned at one end and Logi at the other, they began to eat. Although they met in the middle it was found that Loki had only eaten the flesh leaving the bones, while Logi had consumed not only the flesh with the bones but the trough as well, so the assembly judged Loki the loser.

Utgard-Loki then turned to Thialfi, Thor's servant, and asked him what feat he could perform. He answered that he would run against the fastest member of the giants present. So the king called for the giant Hugi, and all went out of the hall to a nearby plain which the king considered

to be suitable for running upon, and he bid them to run three times. Thialfi had hardly left the starting place before Hugi had completed the course and had returned to meet him. 'You must try harder than that Thialfi', said the king, but he had to admit that there had never been a man in Utgard fleeter of foot than he. In the second race Thialfi was still a bow shot from the finish when Hugi reached it. In the third race when Hugi reached the end, Thialfi had not even gone half-way. All who were witnesses upon the plain agreed that there was no need to run any further races.

So all eyes turned to Thor, who said he would be happy to have a drinking contest with anyone. Utgard-Loki agreed to arrange it, and returning to his hall called for his cupbearer to bring the great drinking horn of Utgard. Presenting the filled horn to Thor he explained that a good drinker might expect to empty the horn in a single draught, some take two and even the most puny of men can always manage it in three.

Thor held the horn, and seeing that it was of no exceptional size, took as long and deep a draught as he was able. At last he set it down and was astonished to discover that the level had scarcely fallen. 'Nothing much to boast of', remarked Utgard-Loki, 'try a second time'. So Thor grasped the horn and raising it to his lips he drank all that he could, but when he looked into the horn a second time he found that he had drunk even less than before. In a great rage, he again tried to consume the contents of the horn but could achieve no better than before. In bitter resignation he returned it to the cupbearer.

'I begin to see that you are not so strong as we thought', said Utgard-Loki. 'If you wish you may try another task, but I doubt that you will succeed.'

'I will try', replied Thor, 'though I am sure that such

draughts as I took would not have been considered small amongst the Aesir. What is the task?'

'It is but a trifling game, which none but our children play. Merely lift my cat from the ground. I would not dare to suggest such a trivial feat if I thought you to be as strong as I have been informed. But as we have all seen here today, you are not what we believed you to be.'

As he spoke a large grey cat walked into the hall. Thor walked up to it and placed his arms around its middle and did all that he could to lift him from the floor, but with all his might he could only raise one paw from the ground. Thor reluctantly gave up and made no further attempt. Utgard-Loki made fun of Thor's feebleness to such an extent that Thor shouted in rage that he would wrestle with anyone present. The king replied that it would be beneath the dignity of any of his subjects do such a thing with one so small, however if he insisted then he could wrestle with his old nurse, Elli. The toothless woman entered the hall of the king and grasped hold of Thor. No matter how hard he tried Thor could not shake off her grip. After a violent struggle Thor began to tire and eventually he was brought to his knees. The king called a halt to the proceedings, saying that if Thor could not overcome the old crone then he had no right to challenge any one of the assembly. He put aside all thoughts of competition and showed the travellers to their seats where they passed the rest of the night in friendship.

The following morning the giant king presented the four with a sumptuous breakfast, taking special care to provide them with all that they could ask for. After the meal he led them to the gate of the city. Once outside Utgard-Loki asked Thor if he thought his journey worthwhile. Thor replied with heavy heart that he could only say that he had brought great shame upon himself, and that he was troubled that he should be called a man of little worth.

'Now,' said the king, 'I shall tell you the truth, as you are beyond the walls of my city, and which you shall never again pass. If I had known sooner of your great strength I should not have permitted you to enter the first time. For I have deceived you with my magic. In the forest, I was the giant called Skrymir. My bag that you failed to open was bound with the strongest of iron rings in such a fashion that none could have loosened them. Even the first of your blows would have been fatal to me had I not set a mountain before me, and now that mountain has three valleys, one of them extremely deep, all made by your hammer.

'Further, when Loki ate as best he could all that was layed before him, it was fire that he competed against, consuming with vigour not only the meat but the trough as well. Hugi, who ran against Thialfi, was really Thought, which is swifter than all runners. When you attempted to empty the horn you performed a remarkable task, for one end of the horn rested in the sea, of which your great draughts lowered to the ebb tide. As for lifting the cat, when you raised its paw from the ground the whole of Utgard shook with fear. What you saw to be a cat was actually the great World Serpent, whose immense body encircles the whole earth, but you almost raised him out of the water. And finally, you managed to hold your own for so long against old age, for that is who Elli was, truly it was no small feat'.

Thor was furiously enraged by the giant king's trickery he would have swung a mighty hammer blow at his head, but Utgard-Loki had disappeared, and where the towering city had stood moments before, there was only a thick heather carpet of purple and green, its glinting dew shimmering merrily to them beneath the morning sun.

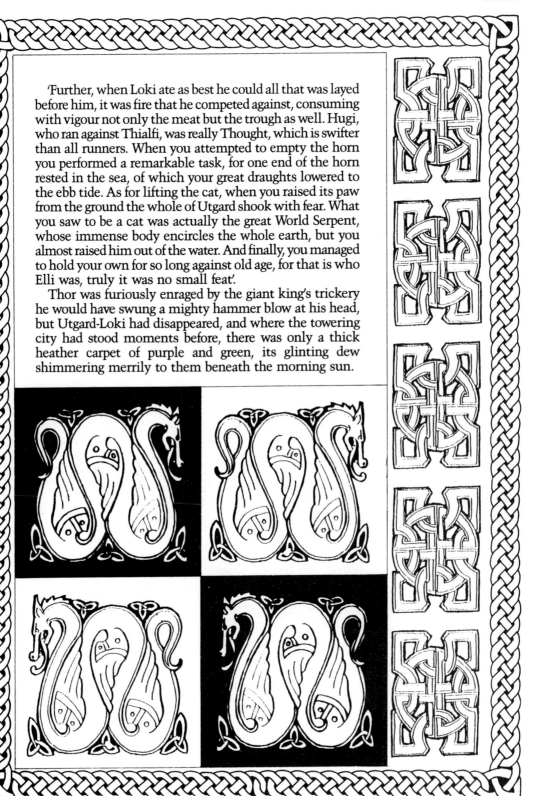

thor and the world serpent

T hor set out early one morning taking time neither to prepare his chariot nor find a companion, such was his haste. He went to Jotunheim in the disguise of a young man. After travelling the whole day in the country of the giants, as evening fell he came to the home of Hymir. Here Thor stayed the night.

In the morning when the giant dragged his fishing boat to the sea edge Thor begged that he might be permitted to join him in his fishing. Hymir said that such a skinny little man could be of no help to him, and added that in all probability all he would catch would be a cold going so far out to sea. Thor was so furious at this that he would have let the giant feel the weight of Mjolnir upon his skull. But controlling his anger he answered politely that he was willing to go as far as the giant wished and he asked what Hymir intended using for bait. Hymir told Thor to find his own bait, so he went to the giant's head of oxen and, taking the head of the largest beast, returned and took his seat in the boat. The giant and Thor rowed the boat together, the giant at the prow and Thor aft, but the god rowed with such powerful strokes that the giant was surprised at the rate at which the boat sped forwards.

Before long they had reached the giant's usual fishing place, but Thor preferred to go further. So they continued rowing until the giant called for him to stop for fear of entering the deep waters of the Iormungandr, the World Serpent. The god continued pulling at the oars and did so for a long while. Finally, when he was satisfied, Thor put up his oars and preparing his line with a good strong hook

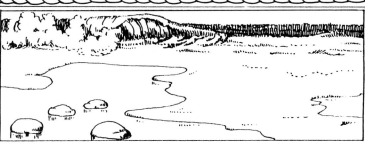

he cast the ox head over the side. Soon the bait was resting on the dark floor of the ocean and then, as Thor had known it would, the World Serpent bit at it greedily. The hook caught deeply in its great gaping mouth. Twisting in pain the serpent dragged violently at the line. The cord held strong but Thor needed both hands to keep his prize from escaping. Then summoning all his might the god pulled so hard that both of his feet were driven through the floor of the boat into the sea below.

Amidst the drenching spray and the incoming water the giant turned pale and cowered away from Thor. The World Serpent in all its fury raised up above the churning waters, breathing out streams of venom upon the wild-eyed god. Just as Thor raised up his hammer to kill the serpent, the giant drew his knife and swung at the taut quivering line. It split with a resounding crack. The serpent released from Thor's hands fell backwards, sliding from view beneath the turbulent waves.

In one last desperate effort to slay the creature Thor hurled his hammer after it, but whether it reached its mark he knew not. In his anger for letting Iormungandr escape he dealt the giant a fearful blow with his gauntleted fist throwing him into the sea. Then leaving the sinking boat far behind he waded with powerful strides back to the shore.

thor's duel

Flying through the air one day on his eight-legged horse Sleipnir, Odin was observed from below by the giant, Hrungnir. The giant called to him proposing a race, for he was certain that his own steed, Gullfaxi, would be able to run faster than Sleipnir.

The race began but Hrungnir, while concentrating upon overtaking Odin, failed to see that he was racing towards the high walls of Asgard. Only when he had passed through the gates did he discover his predicament. He paled with fear. By entering into the realm of the gods, the giant's mortal enemies, he had unwittingly placed his life in danger.

The gods were above taking their enemy at a disadvantage, and rather than do him harm they welcomed him with a sumptuous banquet. The giant relaxed and made the most of his good fortune. He busied himself with consuming the vast quantities of food and mead brought before him.

Presently the drink began to have effect and soon he was boasting of his powers, saying that he would take possession of Asgard and destroy the Aesir, all except the goddesses Freya and Sif, for whom he had other intentions. The gods, seeing that he was not responsible for his words, let him speak saying nothing against him. But Thor, entering the meal hall just as Hrungnir was threatening to carry off his beloved wife Sif, erupted instantly into a thunderous rage. He would have killed the giant there and then if the other gods had not held him back. They begged him to observe the rights of an honoured guest. Thor was at last persuaded to curb his anger, but he challenged the giant to a duel, insisting that he name the time and place.

Three days later the giant stood waiting for Thor beneath the dank, grey, overcast sky. His aid, Mokerkialfi, stood by him. He was a monstrous creature made of clay by the giant's companions in Jotunheim. Hrungnir had prepared himself well with a flint head and heart, and was armed with a shield and club of the same material. Coming towards him was Thor's servant Thialfi, and soon after a terrible rumbling was heard. The giant, at the prompting of Thialfi, thought Thor would attack him from below, and was somehow tunnelling through the earth that very instant, so to protect himself he stood upon his shield.

As Mokerkialfi attacked Thialfi, Hrungnir saw his mistake. Thor came rushing at him from another direction and flung his hammer forcefully at his head. Hrungnir tried to parry the flying hammer with his club, but it was shattered into a thousand fragments which flew out in all directions. One of the fragments struck Thor in the centre of his forehead, bringing him to the ground. But his hammer travelled on, crashing into the giant's head and killing him outright. Hrungnir collapsed to the earth so close to Thor that one of his massive legs lay over the fallen god.

Thialfi, who had by this time successfully subdued the creature of clay, ran to Thor's side. He called all the gods to help lift the giant's leg and free Thor, but even together their strength was not equal to the task. While they were stood about considering how to move the giant, Thor's young three-year-old son Magni appeared. He took the giant's foot in his small hands and heaved him to one side. As a reward for his help Thor presented his son with Gullfaxi, the dead giant's horse.

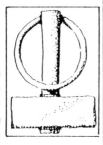

Thor returned home with his son still bearing the sharp flint splinter in his forehead, but no matter how Sif tried she could not remove the obstinate stone. So the goddess called for her friend the witch, Groa (green making), who was noted for her skill in charms and incantations. Immediately the witch came to her aid and began to work her magic, burning in a silver dish rare herbs collected from dark and secret places, and chanting ancient rhymes in her cracked aged voice, slowly she circled the expectant Thor, weaving powerful runes upon the air. The smouldering leaves gave up their subtle odour and the room began to grow small and dark as it filled with the perfumed smoke.

Points of light flickered upon Thor's wide and furrowed brow, bejewelling his ruddy face, and shadows danced unseen against the earthen floor. The stone loosened against the bone and Thor could feel its movement against his skin. He cried out with relief, promising the witch all manner of wealth and wondrous gifts. In his excitement at his pending release, he told her how he had recently crossed the frozen rivers of Elivagar, to rescue her child Orvandil (germ of life) from the hands of the frost giants. He went on and told of how he carried him off in a basket, but the child pushed one of his bare toes out through a hole and it had been bitten by the cruel frost, and Thor, accidentally breaking it off, had cast it up into the night sky to shine brightly and be known as the star Orvandil's Toe.

The old witch was overjoyed with this welcome news and she stopped in the middle of her spell to thank the god, but when she tried to begin again she could not recall precisely where she had left off. So the lights dimmed, the perfume faded, and the smoke drifted out through the hole in the roof. Her spell was broken, the magic spoiled, leaving the stone held faster than ever.

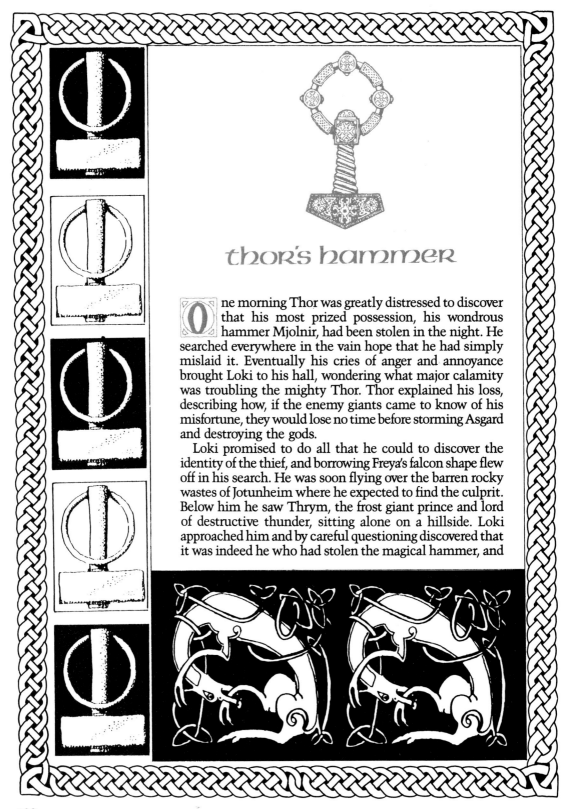

thor's hammer

One morning Thor was greatly distressed to discover that his most prized possession, his wondrous hammer Mjolnir, had been stolen in the night. He searched everywhere in the vain hope that he had simply mislaid it. Eventually his cries of anger and annoyance brought Loki to his hall, wondering what major calamity was troubling the mighty Thor. Thor explained his loss, describing how, if the enemy giants came to know of his misfortune, they would lose no time before storming Asgard and destroying the gods.

Loki promised to do all that he could to discover the identity of the thief, and borrowing Freya's falcon shape flew off in his search. He was soon flying over the barren rocky wastes of Jotunheim where he expected to find the culprit. Below him he saw Thrym, the frost giant prince and lord of destructive thunder, sitting alone on a hillside. Loki approached him and by careful questioning discovered that it was indeed he who had stolen the magical hammer, and

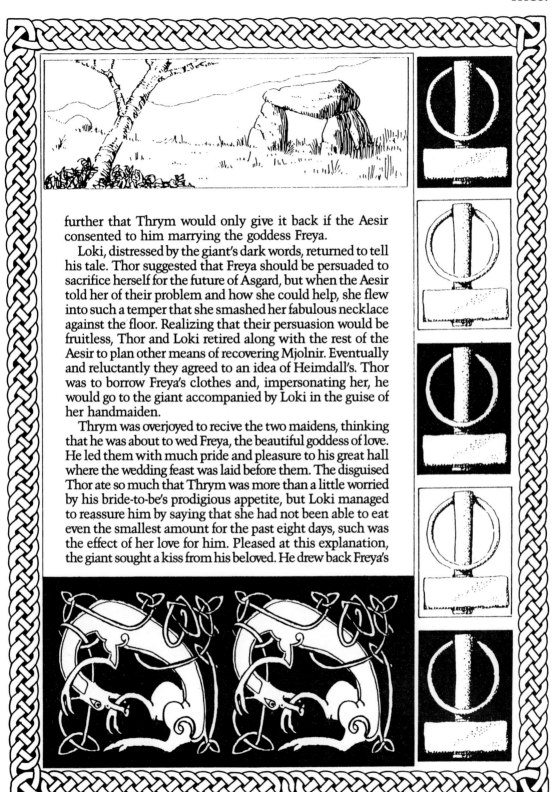

further that Thrym would only give it back if the Aesir consented to him marrying the goddess Freya.

Loki, distressed by the giant's dark words, returned to tell his tale. Thor suggested that Freya should be persuaded to sacrifice herself for the future of Asgard, but when the Aesir told her of their problem and how she could help, she flew into such a temper that she smashed her fabulous necklace against the floor. Realizing that their persuasion would be fruitless, Thor and Loki retired along with the rest of the Aesir to plan other means of recovering Mjolnir. Eventually and reluctantly they agreed to an idea of Heimdall's. Thor was to borrow Freya's clothes and, impersonating her, he would go to the giant accompanied by Loki in the guise of her handmaiden.

Thrym was overjoyed to recive the two maidens, thinking that he was about to wed Freya, the beautiful goddess of love. He led them with much pride and pleasure to his great hall where the wedding feast was laid before them. The disguised Thor ate so much that Thrym was more than a little worried by his bride-to-be's prodigious appetite, but Loki managed to reassure him by saying that she had not been able to eat even the smallest amount for the past eight days, such was the effect of her love for him. Pleased at this explanation, the giant sought a kiss from his beloved. He drew back Freya's

veil and was shocked at the sight of the burning red eyes that stared out at him, but Loki passed this off by saying that she had not slept for eight nights such was her longing for him. Again the giant was satisfied by the quick-witted god's explanation.

The giant had been drinking heavily and was no longer in complete command of his senses when Loki suggested that perhaps the time had come for the marriage ceremony. Drunk with passion and mead he fervently agreed, calling his manservant to bring the sacred hammer to bless the union. As soon as the hammer was presented Thrym took it and laid it in his future wife's lap. With a sigh of relief Thor's mighty hand grasped the handle firmly. In moments the giant and all his followers lay dead around the wedding table, slain by the revengeful Thor.

The two gods hastily left the shattered ruins of Thrym's hall behind them and travelled quickly back to the waiting Aesir, where Thor was glad at last to return his unmanly disguise to Freya.

Some time later when Odin sat upon his high seat Hlidskialf, he looked towards that part of Jotunheim where Thrym had lived and found it to be covered with young green shoots. Thor had taken possession of the place, which from that day on was no longer a land of desolate waste.

thor and geírrod

way adventuring in the shape of a falcon, Loki flew over the hills of Jotunheim. He rested for a time on the roof of the giant Geirrod's house. When the giant saw him, he commanded one of his servants to capture the bird. Seeing the servant's clumsy efforts. Loki amused himself by hopping from place to place, defiantly teasing him, always keeping slightly beyond the reach of the giant's outstretched hand. But suddenly, misjudging his reach, he was caught.

Geirrod inspected the bird closely and soon realized that he held in his powerful grip not a bird but a disguised god. Finding that he could not be induced to speak the giant locked the bird in a cage, and held him there without food or drink for three long months. Eventually Loki was forced through hunger and thirst to reveal who he was. He obtained his release by promising to bring Thor to the giant without the protection of his hammer, his belt of strength or his magical gauntlets.

Returning to the land of the gods, Loki deceived Thor, telling him of the giant's generosity and fine hospitality. He

added that Geirrod had instructed him to convey to Thor an invitation saying that he should be greatly honoured if he, the renowned champion of the gods, would visit his humble hall. So Thor, tricked by Loki's flattering speech, set out on a friendly journey to Jotunheim, leaving his weapons at home.

Before they had gone far, they passed by the hut of the giantess Grid, who was one of Odin's wives. She was horrified to see him so ill-prepared. Along with a warning to beware of treachery, she insisted that he borrow her own belt, staff and gloves.

Some time later they came to the river Veimer. There was no bridge or ford to be found so Thor waded into the water with Loki grasping tightly to his belt. Half-way across the waters unexpectedly quickened, the river rose and began to roar. Amidst the deafening torrent Thor supported himself against Grid's staff, but the current was so powerful that he was in grave danger of being swept away.

Looking about him for a means of escape he glimpsed Gialp, Geirrod's daughter, upstream. Correctly guessing that she had caused the flood he pulled a stone up from the river bed and flung it at her. At the sight of the flying stone the giantess ran for cover and left the river to return to a gentle flow. Reaching the other bank he was so exhausted that he

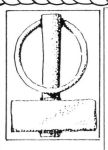

had to pull wearily against a tree to lift himself and Loki out of the river.

They rested for a while and then set off to walk the short distance to the giant's hall. As there was no one to greet them when they arrived they made themselves comfortable. Thor was still tired, so taking the only seat he sat back and stretched his aching legs before him. Suddenly the chair began to move, rising upwards quickly from beneath him. Thor was lifted towards the roof of the hall. Afraid that he should be crushed against the rafters, he pressed Grid's staff against one of the strong oak beams and pushed downwards with all the strength that he could muster. As he forced the chair back to the floor, fearful cries came from underneath him, followed by moans of pain. When he looked under his chair he found the broken bodies of the giant's two daughters Gialp and Greip, who had hidden there planning to murder him.

Finally Geirrod himself entered the hall, and challenged the god to a trial of strength. Before Thor was able to reply the treacherous giant hurled a red-hot ingot directly at him. Thor raised his hand instantly and with the glove of Grid caught the glowing object and threw it back at the giant, who ran for cover behind a broad wooden pillar. The missile shot straight through the wood, such was the power of the throw. It then shot through the cowering giant behind the pillar, and onwards breaking through the outer wall of the hall and eventually buried itself deep in the grassy hillside beyond.

síf's golden haír

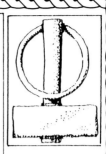

One morning Thor awoke to the tearful cries of his wife Sif. During the night her long golden hair had been stolen, cut from her head as she slept. Thor was angered at this outrage, and he set off to find Loki whom he rightly assumed was behind the evil deed.

Loki tried to escape, but Thor soon caught him and held him in his powerful arms. Dragged before Odin and Frey, Loki begged forgiveness and promised to find for Sif a new head of hair, one that would far outshine that which she had lost. The gods said that they would give him a chance to earn forgiveness, but if he failed in his task then his punishment would be most severe. So Loki hastened to Svartalfheim, the land of the dark elves. There he found Dvalin and implored him to fashion the new hair for Sif. He also asked for gifts to Odin and Frey, hoping to win back their good will.

Soon the dwarf made the spear Gungnir, which always found its target, and also the ship Skidbladnir which had many wonderful powers. Finally he made the golden hair from the finest golden thread, promising that as soon as it touched Sif's head it would begin to grow just as naturally as her original hair had done.

Loki was impressed by the dwarf's work and he declared him to be the most skilled smith in Svartalfheim. His words however were overheard by the brothers Brock and Sindri, who claimed that they could make gifts that would easily outmatch those of Dvalin in both beauty and magical power.

Loki challenged them to prove their boast, rashly wagering his own head against their skill. So the dwarfs began; Brock worked the bellows of the forge and Sindri, fashioning the gold, instructed his brother not to stop the flow of air for even a moment such was the delicacy of his work. Loki, in the shape of a fly, bit Brock in an attempt to distract him from his task, but he continued in spite of this irritation, and soon Sindri drew a fine golden boar named Gullinbursti from the flames.

The dwarf put more gold into the fire and gave instructions to his brother to continue blowing until he had finished. A second time Loki tried to distract Brock and a second time

he was unsuccessful; Sindri pulled from the fire the magic ring named Draupnir, which had the power to generate eight other rings of equal size and weight every ninth night.

Finally Sindri cast a bar of iron into the fire and a third time told his brother to blow until he had finished. In a final effort of desperation Loki, still in the form of a fly, stung Brock so deeply above the eye that his blood flowed and prevented him from seeing what he was doing. Quickly he raised his hands to wipe the blood aside and returned to the bellows. When Sindri came to pull out his work from the fire he was disappointed, he had fashioned a hammer but due to the interruption it was a little short in the handle.

Returning to Asgard the gifts were presented to the gods. From Loki, Odin received the spear Gungnir, Frey accepted the ship Skidbladnir and to Sif he gave the golden hair. Sindri in turn gave Odin the ring Draupnir, Frey the boar Gullinbursti, and Thor the hammer Mjolnir. After due consideration the gods declared the hammer made by Sindri to be of the most worth, for even though it was short in the shaft, in Thor's capable hands it was sure to serve them well.

Loki, loosing his wager, fled to save his head, but he was soon caught by Thor who gave him to Sindri with a warning that although Loki's head might be his to do with what he wished, he must not harm any part of his neck so, restricted in his vengeance, the dwarf contented himself with sewing up Loki's troublesome mouth.

ULLER

Uller was the god of winter, the son of Sif and stepson of Thor. He travelled amongst the cold Northern mountains wrapped in furs, his snow-shoes leaving unmistakable tracks behind him as he hunted, armed with a massive bow. His bow was made of yew and he lived in a vale of yews, a place called Ydalir. In addition to this bow and many arrows he also carried a strong shield and was indeed known as the shield god. As such he was invoked by those about to do battle, to provide them with protection from enemy weapons.

heimdall

Known as the White God, Heimdall was the watchman of the Aesir. Day in, day out, he would look out over the Rainbow Bridge, waiting for Ragnarok, the final hour when the enemies of the gods would come rushing across to invade Asgard. He required less sleep than a bird, so he never tired in his vigil. His hearing was so keen that he could detect the sound of grass growing on the hillsides and wool upon a sheep's back. Such was his sight that he could see a hundred miles by night or day. It was because of these attributes that he was chosen by the gods to be their watchman.

He was the son of Odin but had nine mothers. They were beautiful giantesses, the nine Wave Maidens, their names were Gialp, Greip, Egia, Augeia, Augiafa, Sindur, Atla, Iarnsaxa and Ulfrun. Together the sisters looked after young Heimdall, who grew rapidly, nourished upon the moisture of the waves and the warmth of the sun. Soon he was strong enough to leave them and join his father in Asgard.

When he arrived he found the gods had just completed the construction of Bifrost, the Rainbow Bridge. From its source amongst the roots of Yggdrasil and close to Mimir's Well, it spanned the gap between Midgard and Asgard. The slender arch was made of the red of burning fire, the blue of the clear air and the green of the watery depths. But the gods, looking upon their fine work, were afraid that the frost giants should leave their icy homes in Jotunheim, pass over the bridge and attack them. So, after due consideration, Heimdall was chosen to watch the crossing. For the task he was armed with a bright sword and to warn the gods of any threatening approach he was given a horn named Giallarhorn, whose blast would echo throughout all the nine worlds. From where he stood at the rainbow's end, Heimdall would either hang the horn from a low branch of the World Tree or else rest it in the waters of Mimir's Well.

Situated at the highest point of the bridge was his long hall, Himinbiorg. Here he would sit dressed in his fine white

armour, while outside his golden-maned horse Gulltop would stand waiting. With Bragi, he welcomed heroes to Valhalla. He was also known as Riger and Gullintani (golden toothed), because of his radiant smile.

Riger

eaving Bifrost in the care of the other gods, Heimdall set out to travel upon the earth. He rode Gulltop far along the seashore, through the wind-blown spray and beneath the calling gulls. Turning from the sea, he followed a path which led him amongst broad dunes, crowned with long dark grass which swayed gently above the silver sand. Before long the path brought him to a rough hut, made of cut turf and sun-bleached driftwood.

Seated inside tending their small crackling fire, he found an old couple, Ai (great grandfather) and his loving wife Edda (great grandmother). As soon as they saw the stranger, they offered him a portion of their meagre meal of porridge, begging him to stay and share their hospitality. Heimdall gratefully accepted their invitation and, giving his name as Riger, stayed with them for a full three days. He taught them many things during this time, but eventually he had to leave and continue his journey.

Some time later Edda gave birth to a son. Short, dark-skinned and strong, they named him Thrall. As he grew, he showed a great capacity for work of all kinds. When he became of age he married a girl called Thyr, strong like himself with tanned skin and flat feet. Together they worked long hours, starting early and finishing late. They had many

children and from them all the thralls or serfs of the Northern lands are descended.

Leaving Ai and Edda, Heimdall rode further inland and found well-tendered fields and a strongly built farmhouse. Inside he was welcomed by Afi (grandfather) and Amma (grandmother), who invited him to sit with them and share their plain but plentiful meal. He was glad to accept and remained with them three days and three nights. In return for their hospitality he instructed them in all manner of things.

Some time after his departure, Amma bore a son called Karl, he was strong and he was wise. When he grew up he displayed great aptitude for agricultural matters and married a thrifty wife named Snor. Together their farm grew and prospered, and from them all husbandmen are descended.

After his stay at the farmhouse Heimdall continued his journey. Finally, after several days, he climbed a hill. Around its summit a strong wall had been built. Here he was welcomed by Fadir (father) and Modir (mother). Dressed in rich clothes, they greeted him with gentle words and polite conversation. Before him on the carved oak table they set expensive wines in silver goblets and exotic food upon costly dishes. They remained together for three days until the time came to depart.

Before long Modir had a son named Jarl, who grew to love the hunt and showed great skill at arms. He was learned and well-spoken, achieving acts of great valour which brought fame and renown to his name. He married Erna and she bore him many children, who became the ancestors of all rulers of men. Their youngest, Konur, was destined to become the first king of Denmark.

Loki and Freya

Through the darkness of the night Heimdall heard a sound. It was soft to the ear, but of such a nature to raise his interest. In the direction of Folkvang, Freya's sleeping hall, someone was moving quietly. Heimdall's sight cut like an ashen spear through the barrier of darkness. He saw Loki creeping with great stealth about the hall in the shape of a fly. Resuming his common form Loki stood at the side of Freya's bed. He watched her as she slept, his eyes thirsting for her costly golden necklace, Brisingamen.

The White God saw that the thief would not be able to take the necklace without disturbing Freya's slumber, but he suddenly grew alarmed when Loki began quickly to mutter runes. As he did so his form began to change — rapidly his size diminished until he could hardly be seen. Then, in the shape of a flea, he entered the goddess's bed, and biting her on the side he caused her to turn over but took care that he did not wake her. Then returning to his natural shape he carefully removed the jewel and left the hall as quickly as he could.

Instantly Heimdall set off in pursuit of the treacherous thief. As he reached Loki's side Heimdall drew his gleaming sword and would have cut him down, but Loki transformed himself into a flickering blue flame and the sword flashed through the air with no effect. So Heimdall in reply changed into a cloud, heavy with rain and sent a stream of water cascading down upon the flame. Loki immediately became a bear and opened his jaws wide to catch the falling rain.

Heimdall likewise assumed the form of a bear and fell against Loki with a tremendous force, knocking him heavily to the ground. Together in the darkness they fought. Tooth against tooth and claw against claw, they rolled and tumbled as wild beasts. Loki did not fare well and changed again, becoming a seal he tried to escape to the sea. However Heimdall followed him in the same shape. Finally catching hold of Loki, he overpowered him and forced him to relinquish the stolen gold.

Heimdall returned to Asgard and in the hall of Folkvang he found Freya waiting anxiously. With a grateful heart she accepted the return of her precious Brisingamen.

hel

el was the dark child of Loki and the daughter of Angurboda. She was therefore the sister of both Fenris the wolf, and Iormungandr the World Serpent. Her body was half whole and half rotting flesh. Odin gave her the kingdom of Niflheim, the land of the dead that lay deep within the earth. Far to the North its boundary was the river Gioll, crossed only by a slender bridge guarded by the grim Modgud. At the Hel gate waited the fearsome hound Garm, watching from his dark cave Gnipa. Within Niflheim was the pool of Hvergelmir, from which flowed the 12 streams known as Elivagar.

Hel's dismal hall was called Elvidner (misery). Upon her table was a dish called Hunger and a knife named Starvation. Delay was her house slave and Sloth her bondmaid, her threshold was Precipice and Care was her bed. Burning Anguish decorated her walls. To this place came not only all manner of criminals, murderers, adulterers and perjurers, but also those who died a bloodless death of sickness or old age.

Also within her kingdom was Nastrond (strand of corpses). It was a vast hall constructed of a wickerwork of woven snakes. Their heads turned inwards continually flooding the hall and its luckless inhabitants with venom. Before reaching the hall the river Slithr, with its unceasing flow of sharp sword blades, first had to be waded.

Occasionally Hel would leave her dark realm to ride the earth upon her pale three-legged horse. Wherever she went fame and pestilence were sure to follow — she brought misery and death in her wake.

íдun

I dun was the goddess of spring. She came to Asgard with her husband Bragi, and brought with her a casket which was forever full of the wonderful apples which provided all who received them with eternal youth. Because of these apples the gods were free from the effects of time and never aged.

the stolen apples

O ne day, Odin, Loki and Hoenir were travelling through a broad valley rich in vegetation. They were hungry and without food of any sort. Presently they came upon a herd of oxen, and taking one of the beasts they killed it and prepared its flesh for the pot. But they found it impossible to boil. Every time they lifted the lid from the pot and looked inside they saw that the meat remained uncooked. They sat about their fire pondering upon the situation when a sound was heard above them. Looking up they saw a gigantic eagle perched on the top-most branch of an ageing ivy-strewn oak tree.

The eagle spoke to them and admitted that he had used magic to prevent the meat cooking. He then said that if they shared it with him, he would remove the spell. The gods were happy to agree to his conditions and the meal was soon ready. They were just about to divide it between them when suddenly the eagle flew down and snatched three quarters of the ox for himself. Annoyed and considering this to be more than his fair share, Loki grabbed a joint of meat and struck the eagle across the back.

Loki soon discovered his mistake for this was no ordinary bird, but an infamous giant by the name of Thjassi wearing his coat of feathers. The joint of meat stuck fast to the giant's feathered back and also to the god's own hand and try as

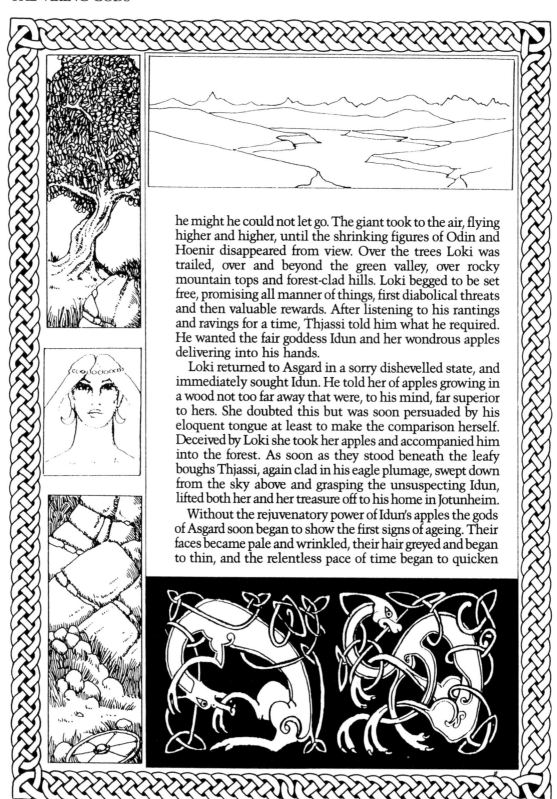

he might he could not let go. The giant took to the air, flying higher and higher, until the shrinking figures of Odin and Hoenir disappeared from view. Over the trees Loki was trailed, over and beyond the green valley, over rocky mountain tops and forest-clad hills. Loki begged to be set free, promising all manner of things, first diabolical threats and then valuable rewards. After listening to his rantings and ravings for a time, Thjassi told him what he required. He wanted the fair goddess Idun and her wondrous apples delivering into his hands.

Loki returned to Asgard in a sorry dishevelled state, and immediately sought Idun. He told her of apples growing in a wood not too far away that were, to his mind, far superior to hers. She doubted this but was soon persuaded by his eloquent tongue at least to make the comparison herself. Deceived by Loki she took her apples and accompanied him into the forest. As soon as they stood beneath the leafy boughs Thjassi, again clad in his eagle plumage, swept down from the sky above and grasping the unsuspecting Idun, lifted both her and her treasure off to his home in Jotunheim.

Without the rejuvenatory power of Idun's apples the gods of Asgard soon began to show the first signs of ageing. Their faces became pale and wrinkled, their hair greyed and began to thin, and the relentless pace of time began to quicken

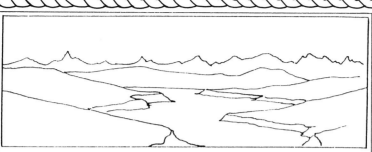

for them. They soon discovered that Loki, as usual, was behind their misfortune, so they threatened him with a terrible punishment if he could not conceive some method of regaining their beloved Idun and her precious apples of youth. Alarmed, Loki borrowed Freya's falcon shape and flew to Jotunheim. On reaching Thjassi's hall he found that the giant was not at home. Searching through the giant's hall Loki discovered the delighted Idun. Changing her into a sparrow he flew off with her carefully held between his sharp talons.

In time Thjassi returned and immediately realizing what had happened took off in pursuit of the falcon-clothed god.

The Aesir waiting anxiously on the walls of Asgard saw Loki approaching in the distance. Closely behind him flew the dark form of the eagle. Loki came nearer to Asgard, but the large eagle was gaining on him with tremendous speed. Loki soared over the walls with Idun and was only moments away from disaster as Thjassi prepared to overtake them. Seeing this the gods acted quickly; they piled dry wood upon the walls which they set aflame the instant Loki passed overhead. The raging fire shot skywards. The giant had no time to avoid his fate and flying into the flames he singed the tips of his wing feathers. He fell clumsily to earth and the awaiting gods, where he was swiftly slain by the Aesir.

Thjassi had a daughter named Skadi and when she heard of her father's death she rushed to Asgard ready to avenge him. The gods accepted responsibility for the killing and offered one of their number as a husband, further promising that they should make her laugh. This was something which she had never done before and considered beyond all their godly powers to achieve. However, she agreed to their proposal.

To make her choice of a husband Skadi was not allowed to see the faces of the gods but only their feet. Inspecting the row of feet set before her she decided upon the pair she considered to be of the most handsome proportions, being sure that they would be the feet of Balder. They were however those of Niord, and he became her husband.

At the wedding feast Loki, by playing the fool, managed to make the stern-faced giantess smile and eventually as the night went on she began to laugh, leaving the gods' bargain satisfied. Finally, to commemorate her father, Odin took Thjassi's eyes and threw them high up into the night sky were they shone as stars for all to see.

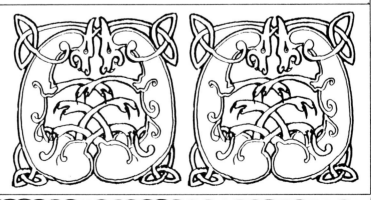

forseti

F orseti, the son of Balder and Nanna, was the god of justice amongst the Aesir. He was renowned for his great wisdom and wise council. In Glitnir, his hall of golden walls and silver roof, he would settle the disputes of gods and men. His aid was sought by all who were about to enter a court of justice. Oaths were sworn in his name that none dared break for fear of incurring his displeasure.

forseti's story

The Asegeir were the 12 wisest men of the Frisians. Their king called upon them to go out into the land and collect the laws of the people, and from these laws they should form a structured code of law for all the country. So they travelled from farm to farm, and village to village, carefully recording the laws of the people. When the collection was complete they set off in a small boat to find a secluded place where they would be able to work at their task undisturbed.

No sooner had they embarked, however, when a terrible storm arose which drove their small vessel far out to sea. The storm raged on, the wind-driven waves constantly threatening to swamp their craft, until they discovered that they had completely lost their bearings. In their distress they called upon the god Forseti to come to their aid. As they came to the end of their prayer the storm ceased and looking about them they discovered that the boat now held a 13th passenger.

The stranger quickly grasped the rudder and steered the boat to a small island. They were gratefully relieved to be able to scramble to the safety of the shore. Standing around in silence, they were unable to speak as the stranger threw his mighty battle axe. It struck a nearby mound where a bright spring immediately began to flow. The company followed his example by drinking the spring's refreshing waters. The stranger gestured them to sit in a circle and now they had a chance to look at him more closely. The men were astonished at how much he looked like each of them in some way but like none of them as a whole.

After a time the stranger broke the silence and began to speak. In a careful and steady tone he pronounced a full and balanced code of laws which contained all the best points of those the Asegeir had collected. Then as suddenly as he had appeared he was gone from their midst.

Immediately the assembly found that they could speak once more and each exclaimed that it was Forseti himself who had been amongst them and had provided a set of just laws by which their people should be judged. To commemorate the god's visit they declared the island to be a sacred place and called it Heligoland (Holy Land).

valí

Vali was the son of Odin by the princess Rinda. He shared with his father the hall Valaskialf and sat as one of the 12 gods in the Hall of Gladsheim. He was one of the gods who survived Ragnarok to rule over the new earth.

He was represented as an archer and has links with the Christian St Valentine who was also an archer. Both were associated with a period of the year between the middle of January and the middle of February. It was with Vali's own bow and arrow that he killed his brother, the god Hodur; this was his revenge for the death of Balder, another of the sons of Odin. As Balder was killed at the midwinter solstice, it is only fitting that his avenger should be linked with this early part of the year.

the Bírth of valí

Enemy forces were assembled at the borders of the Land of the Ruthenes. Their king, Billing, was a troubled man. He was too old to fight and his only child, a daughter, refused to marry, thus denying him of the much needed support of a warrior son-in-law.

Billing was sat in his hall considering both his own sad future and that of his people, when an unexpected stranger entered. He was a tall man, wearing a long cloak of woad blue and a large soft hat, its broad brim hanging low, almost concealing his face. The newcomer asked the king why he was so down-hearted — indeed, he enquired in such a concerned manner that the king was happy to confide all. Upon hearing his story the stranger volunteered to lead the entire army of the king against his enemy.

It was not long before the stranger returned victorious from the battlefield, Billing's foes vanquished and his army triumphant. As a reward for his services the stranger asked

for Rinda's hand in marriage and the king, eager to bring such a courageous and worthy warrior into his household, gladly gave his warmest consent. However when he proudly presented himself to the princess his proposal was rejected with scorn, and when he attempted to kiss her she hit him heavily about the head.

Odin, for he was the stranger, departed hurt and dejected. Later he returned disguised as a metal smith, calling himself Rosterus. Brought before the king he fashioned many wonderful and precious things; armbands of radiant gold, brooches of shining silver and all manner of glittering jewel-studded ornaments. The king was so delighted with the man's spectacular skill that he happily agreed to his request to marry the princess Rinda. But the princess had even less time for the smith than she had for the stranger in blue, and a second time Odin's head rang with the force of her angry blows.

When Odin came a third time to the king's hall, in the guise of a handsome and youthful warrior, he was again rejected by the obstinate Rinda. He became so bitterly enraged at this triple insult that he raised his rune staff. He furiously pointed it at the princess, casting such a spell that she fell down apparently dead.

When Rinda finally awoke, King Billing and all his courtiers were thrown into great sadness for it was discovered that the princess had completely lost her senses. He called his advisors and he called all his most trusted healers, but between them with all their wisdom and knowledge, they could do nothing to help her. Eventually an old woman named Vecha appeared at the king's door and offered to cure the princess. First she instructed that her feet should be washed, but this had little effect, so then she promised better and more effective treatment. She commanded all those present in the princess's chamber to leave. When she was at last alone with Rinda the old woman took her normal shape, for she was Odin in disguise. Then binding her securely and releasing her from his spell, he made her promise to become his wife. Realizing that she had little choice Rinda reluctantly agreed. After a time she gave birth to a son who was named Vali.

VÍÐAR

Odin the one-eyed god fell in love with a beautiful giantess called Gird and she became his wife. Their child was the strong and silent Vidar. His home was Landvidi, which lay in the midst of an ancient and almost impenetrable forest. It was a place of powerfully-scented flowers and lush greenery, a place of deep natural silence.

Odin took his young son to the Well of Urd, where he questioned the Norns concerning Vidar's destiny. They answered in mysterious riddles, but when their words were explained it was revealed that at Ragnarok Vidar was to avenge his father's death and live on into the new age following the fall of the old gods.

Ragnarok

the Death of Balder

Autumn came to an end and the first mild snows of winter began to fall. The gods noticed how Balder's once happy and cheerful face had become unusually clouded. The bright god was troubled; he had been repeatedly distressed by a terrible dream, an ominous warning of great danger to his life. He told the Aesir of his tormenting visions and they swore that everything possible would be done to protect him from the threatening hand of fate.

Frigga sought oaths from all things asking that none should dare to harm Balder her son. Over the winter hills she went receiving the assurance of fire, water, air and earth, of gold, silver and all other metals, of diseases and poisons, of birds, beasts and all living things, begging that all would abide by her will. So great was their love for the bright god that all of creation was happy to swear to the oath.

Balder became happy once more and his dark dreams faded from memory. From that time on whenever the gods met together, it became a favourite pastime to have Balder stand before them while they hurled missiles at him. Whether they were balls of snow, stones or spears none would harm him, nor would sharp-edged swords or polished

battleaxes, even when directed against him with skill and strength.

The gods were greatly entertained with their sport, all that was except Loki. Jealous of Balder's popularity it angered him that the White God was not hurt. He went to Fensalir, the hall of Frigga, disguised as an old woman collecting sticks for her fire. There he found the mother of the gods and joined her in conversation. As time passed Frigga asked the old woman if she knew what the gods were doing at their assembly. Loki replied that they were indulging in a dangerous game attacking Balder. Frigga explained that all things had promised not to harm Balder so he was quite safe. Then Loki asked if everything upon or within the earth had made his promise. The goddess replied that all things but one had sworn, for there was a plant, mistletoe, that was too young to be bound by an oath. As soon as Loki heard these words he took his leave of Frigga and assuming his usual form once more, hastened across the frosted land to the eastern side of Valhalla, where the young mistletoe grew upon an ancient tree. Finding the small plant he carefully cut off a piece and returned to the plain where the gods were still enjoying their game.

The blind god Hodur, not being able to take part in their game, was standing away from the rest. When Loki saw this

he approached him and asked why he did not join in with
the others. He answered simply that as he could not see
Balder he was not able to hurl anything at him, and besides
he had nothing to throw. So Loki gave him the twig and
offered to guide his hand. Hodur, pleased at his offer, stepped
into the ring of gods and with Loki's help threw the small
branch at Balder. The mistletoe flew through the air,
spinning as it went, the small white berries flashing like
jewels as they caught the winter sun. Then, striking Balder
on the chest, it pierced his bright body. With a cry of anguish
he sank to the gound. The laughter of the gods ceased
abruptly as he fell, they stood astonished, unable to utter
a sound. Balder's life-blood spilled upon the pure white snow
of Asgard, soaking away into the receptive earth beneath and
silence reigned upon the land.

    Looking upon his lifeless body, the gods angrily called for
vengeance on Hodur, whose hand had perpetrated the deed.
Thor would have killed him instantly but his hand was held,
fearing to desecrate the sacred place where they stood. Balder
was dead. Such was the Aesir's sorrow and grief that the
woeful sound of their lamentations echoed throughout the
nine worlds.

    When Frigga was called to the scene she pleaded for one
of their number to ride down into the very depths of the

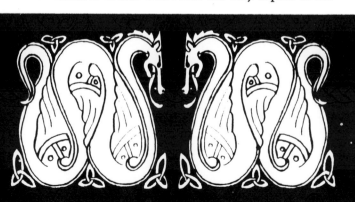

earth. She asked for a messenger to go and search out Hel, the goddess of the dead, and discover what ransom she asked for the release of her captive Balder. Hermod, his brother, came forth and offered to attempt the task and Odin, hoping against hope that a way might be found to outwit the plans of fate, gave him his horse Sleipnir to speed him on his way.

The gods turned back to the dead body and gently carried it in respectful ceremony to a place on the ocean shore where Balder's ship Hringhorn lay upon a shingle beach. The ship was the biggest in the world, so large indeed that the gods were unable to push it into the water, so they sent to Jotunheim for the help of Hyrrokin the giantess. After a time she arrived riding a wolf and using twisted serpents as a bridle. Handing her mount to four of Odin's servants to hold, she went to the ship and with a single push shoved it into the sea. So violent was the movement that sparks shot from the rollers and the earth shook all around. Thor, angered at the giantess's irreverence, grasped his hammer tightly and would have smashed her skull had not the other gods held him back.

Once the vessel was in the water, a funeral pyre was built high upon its wide deck, on which the body of Balder was rested with great care. The gods and goddesses assembled upon the shore to bid farewell to the beloved son of Odin. First came the father of the gods accompanied by Frigga his wife, and the Valkyr host. Overhead the two ravens circled in the clear blue sky, their rough voices calling out a song of lament. Next came Frey in his chariot drawn by the golden boar Gullinbursti. Heimdall rode up on his horse Gulltop closely followed by Freya's chariot drawn by cats. As the other gods arrived so too did a great number of frost giants, many elves and an uncountable hoard of dwarfs, so great was the fame of Balder.

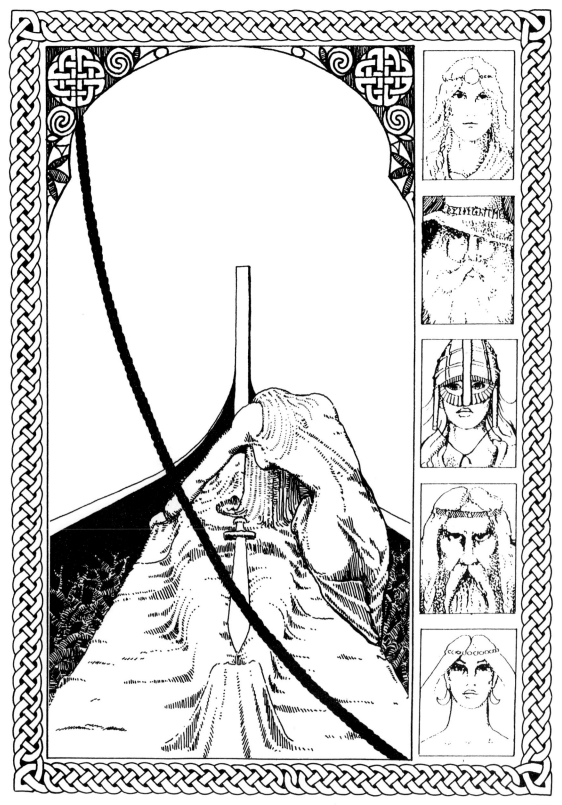

The ceremony began as the day drew to a close, and the sun sank low over the icy sea. Thor raised his hammer and blessed the pyre with hallowed words. Around the cold body, all Balder's possessions were positioned with reverent care. Upon the white God's breast, Odin placed a gift of his own wonderful ring, Draupnir. As the evening sky reddened and the last warming rays of the sun slowly withdrew, leaving the earth to the frozen clutches of night, a torch was put to the pyre. Nanna, Balder's beautiful wife, lay down beside her husband to be consumed with him in the flames. The assembly stood quietly upon the sloping shingle, their soft voices singing the funeral song. With sad faces flickering gold, each was lost in his own grief. The waves carried the great ship far out to sea, flames lapping at the vessel's sides, and burning high against the darkening sky. Odin stood amongst the crowd, tears falling from his blurred eyes. None grieved more than he, for above the loss of a son he foresaw the dark future that Balder's death heralded for Aesir.

the ride to hel

Through dark howling valleys of wind-swept desolation Hermod passed. Rushing over vast wastelands of stunted vegetation and past hideously deformed trees, he hastened to the land of death. Heedless to danger he sped on, splashing through marsh and mire. The grasping mud clung tenaciously to Sleipnir's legs, attempting to drag both horse and rider down into the murky depths of the deadly swamp.

Over dark mountains, fighting constantly against the biting wind they rode, Sleipnir's hooves holding firm upon the shattered rock that formed their perilous path. For nine long days and nine long nights Hermod travelled the road to Hel.

Wailing voices hung on the wind, calling pitifully for him to stop, promising all manner of reward if only he would turn back. At other times he heard the tormented screams and howls of unseen and unimaginable creatures, sometimes far off, sometimes horribly close by.

There were lights too. First he saw them to either side of his path, pale blue flames in the blackness which followed him on a parallel course. Then they came nearer; soon they were dancing before him, faint points of sickly light, glowing brightly then dimming, only to reappear elsewhere. As time passed the lights became stronger forming ghostly shadows of human form, with deep unseeing eyes and hollow gaping mouths. Wearing broken crowns and rusted helmets, their tattered cloaks revealed the ragged remains of once splendid mailcoats. Tortured faces of unknown age displayed faint memories of a long past glory and, as if finding the gaze of living eyes unbearable, they vanished almost as quickly as they appeared.

On and on Hermod and Sleipnir rode, leaving the visions behind them, leaping frozen streams and wading icy rivers. The dark water tore cruelly at their flesh. Upon solid ground again, Sleipnir's snorting breath shot out like jets of steam before them as they galloped.

Finally they came to the great wide river Gjoll, its far bank lay beyond sight in the pitch black distance. Their road of terror led them to a bridge of glittering gold. Sleipnir's hooves rang and clattered against the metal as they crossed. The bridge keeper, a maiden named Modgud, appeared before them and asked Hermod who he was. She told him that on

the previous day, five full companies of slain warriors had passed over the bridge without nearly as much noise as he alone had made. But she saw clearly that he had not the colour of death upon his cheeks, and asked his errand. Hermod answered, telling her of his mission to seek out Hel and negotiate the release of Balder. Modgud recalled Balder's recent passing and showed him the path he took to Hel's dark kingdom.

At last Hermod saw before him the ancient towering gates of Hel. Urging Sleipnir into a gallop he raced at the closed gates, then at the last moment the horse made a tremendous leap and cleared them with ease. Hermod continued to ride the shortest distance to the doors of Hel's palace.

There at Hel's table, amongst the dead, he found Balder seated in the place of honour. Rushing to his brother's side he explained that he had come to take him back to Asgard. But Balder remained unmoved, convinced that he was doomed to stay in Niflheim for ever. The brothers passed the night in deep conversation, recalling past times and remembering the joys of their youth.

The following morning he went to Hel and begged her to allow Balder to accompany him home, assuring her that the whole earth was in mourning at his death. Hel promised that if all things, animate or otherwise, would weep for him, then he would be free to return to Asgard. If however anyone should refuse to weep, then he would have to stay in her realm of death until the end of time.

As Hermod turned to leave, Balder grasped him urgently by the arm and pressed into his hand Odin's gift, the ring Draupnir, to return to his father as a keepsake. Nanna too came forward and presented him with gifts to convey to Frigga, and a finger ring to give to Fulla. With hope in his

heart Hermod took these items, and retracing his steps rode back to the Aesir.

Arriving before the anxiously waiting gods he related all that Hel had said. Immediately they knew what was to be done and sent out messengers to the farthest part of the world, begging all to weep for Balder, to satisfy the conditions of his release.

All things complied with their wishes, all the peoples of the earth, the men of Midgard, the giants of Jotunheim, the elves of Alfheim and the dwarfs of Svartalfheim; and all the plants that grew, all the animals that walked and crawled, the birds of the air and the fish of the sea; even the rocks at the very heart of the world — all were willing to shed tears for the beloved Balder. As the messengers were returning home with the glad news and joy in their hearts, they came to a cave where an old woman named Thaukt was sitting. When they saw her, they asked her to shed a tear for the White God, but she turned at them scowling and said that she would not cry for him, let Hel keep what she had.

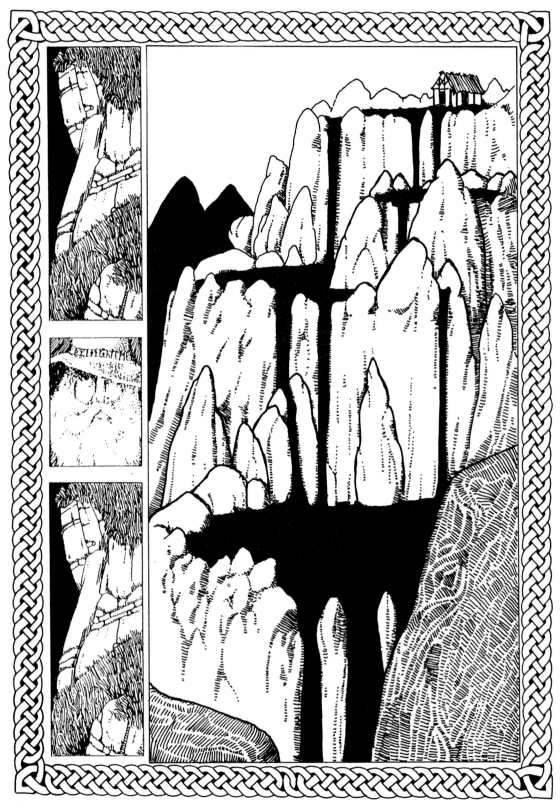

Loki's treachery

The messengers were bewildered by Thaukt's cruel reply, and they travelled back to Asgard in silence. When the gods were told they quickly perceived that the old hag was none other than the treacherous Loki in disguise and they were filled with rage. Immediately they swore to revenge themselves upon the evil god.

Foreseeing the anger of the gods, Loki had already fled, concealing himself within a seldom visited mountain range. In a lofty place he built a house with doors opening on each side so that he could look out in all directions. He would lie in the form of a salmon throughout the day, hidden beneath the cascading torrents of a mountain stream. Alone in the turbulent waters, he would pass time by calculating methods of outwitting the gods in whatever way they should think to capture him.

One day Loki sat in his home toying with flax and yarn. After a time spent trying different ideas he made a fishing net, the first the world had ever seen. But he did not have time to try out his invention because Odin had discovered him, looking down from his seat Hlidskialf, and now Loki saw the Aesir approaching. Quickly he threw his net into the fire and ran to hide in the river.

When the gods came to the house they saw amongst the embers of the fire Loki's invention, and immediately they realized that it must be for catching fish. Thinking that the nearby river would be an ideal place for Loki to hide, they set to work and made a net of the same design as the charred remains. Thor took one end of the net onto the far side of the river while the remainder of the gods held the other end. Slowly they dragged it up stream, but despite taking great care they failed to catch him. The net passed over Loki as he lay still between two stones. However the gods felt that some living thing had touched the net, so having weighted the net they cast it a second time and drew it along, scraping the bottom of the bed and raising clouds of mud as they progressed. Loki, seeing the net draw near, made a mighty leap and jumped over it then he swam off towards the sea. The gods followed him with their net. He had two courses of action available to him: he could either make for the sea, or turn about and pass over the net a second time. He chose to jump. High in the air he leapt, but Thor was quick to act and he caught him in his strong fist.

Having Loki at last under their control the Aesir took him to a deep cavern. There they brought his two sons Vali and Nari. The former they changed into a wolf and in this form he viciously set about his brother, killing him and devouring his body. The gods took the intestines and using them as ropes bound Loki to three heavy rocks. Then came Skadi who hung a snake above him in such a fashion that its venom would drip unceasingly upon his upturned face. The gods departed leaving Sigyn, his faithful wife, standing beside him catching the drops in a dish as they fell. When the dish became full she had to empty it casting the contents to one side, during this time the venom fell upon Loki's face. This caused him great pain and he writhed in agony, twisting so violently that the earth itself shook and trembled.

the twilight of the gods

After Balder's untimely death all the goodness withdrew from the earth letting evil spread over the land. The bleak Fimbul winter arrived, raging across the world with a fury that defied the memory of man. Spring came, but icy winds pinched the young buds and the year's new shoots failed to penetrate the hard frozen soil. Throughout the season of summer, the sun shone only as a feeble white disc, pale beyond the ever present clouds of falling snow. Three terrible winters passed without a single day of summer warmth.

Terrible wars were fought, the like of which had never been seen before. In all countries, in all kingdoms, men driven by the needs of the cold fought against one another. Gaining little or losing all, still they fought as the unrelenting snows fell. Man killed man in three long years of battle and strife. Brother slew brother and father slew son, the ties of kinship were no more.

Amidst the frozen heavens, Skoll the ravenous wolf rose up and opening his jaws wide he devoured the sun, and the moon was likewise consumed by his brother Hati. Darkness descended upon the earth. Observing these wonders with questioning eyes, men saw the stars fall from their alotted positions. They smashed into the earth and the ground shook, causing trees to sway and fall. All around the mountains trembled.

Fenris broke free from his bonds, the magic of the elves having failed at last. The Midgard serpent heaved his

tremendous body from the depths of the ocean, drowning the land with gigantic waves as he cast out a thundering wash of destruction. Upon the churning waters, the ship Naglfar sailed. Made from the uncut nails of dead men, the vessel was steered by Hrym the mighty giant.

Fenris approached Asgard, his snarling lips revealing blood-thirsty teeth. Fire burned brightly in his eyes. The serpent beside him breathed forth a deluge of venom filling both the air above and the waters below with an impenetrable mass of the most deadly poison.

Such was the turmoil that the very heavens were split asunder. Through the gulf strode the ancient Surtur, cutting a vast wake of smouldering devastation, closely followed by his army of fire giants from Muspel. Above him he wielded his flaming sword which cut through the air shining brighter than the sun had ever done. Shadows came shooting from the creature of flame as the darkness fled before him, advancing across the bridge Bifrost, its fragile frame shattered beneath the pounding feet of the giant's army. It splintered into thousands of mirrored fragments, each glinting brightly in the blood-red light.

Loki, lusting for revenge against the gods, rode ahead of the legions of the dead. In full battle dress they marched,

pale corpses, grim-faced beneath ancient iron helmets. Tattered banners and flags before them, harsh cries rang out from cracked horns. Spear and sword clashed rhythmically against shield. Voices sounded in strange tongues and called out long-forgotten battle cries. Beside the host of Loki, Hrym advanced with all the Hrymthusar, the ice giants of the North. On they marched, on to the battlefield of Vigrid.

Seeing the enemy approaching Heimdall grasped the Giallarhorn, and raising it to his lips blew the alarm, that perilous note the gods had for ever feared to hear. Odin hastily took his horse and riding to the Well of Urd urged the Norns to reveal how best to enter into battle against his foes. But the Norns were silent, they gave him no answer. Their faces were concealed and their web lay torn upon the ground.

The great tree shook and the earth moved underfoot, nowhere was safe from the mounting danger. Odin rushed to the field, his spear in his strong hand, a gleaming helmet upon his head. Behind him came the heroes of Valhalla, resplendent in their bright trappings of war. The sons of Muspel stood around the edge of the battlefield, behind them the earth burned in every direction.

Casting his spear high over the heads of the evil host, Odin vibrated his sacred oath for the last time. The battle began. Seeking out Fenris his enemy, the father of the gods drew his sword and engaged him in single combat, bringing cold iron against tooth and claw. Thor standing by his side was unable to assist, as the World Serpent was towering before him.

Frey fought valiantly against Surtur, each striking mighty blows, but Frey had no sword and eventually he fell before the Flame Giant's overwhelming strength.

Garm came running from the distant cave of Gnipa. With pounding feet he rushed at the one-handed Tyr; their fight was fierce. The two were well-matched and both were slain. Thor killed the Midgard serpent, but wearily grasping his wonderous hammer he was engulfed in the monster's venom. Staggering back nine paces he collapsed, never to rise again.

Odin fell, his body broken by the fearsome jaws of the monsterous wolf. As Fenris howled with the pleasure of victory, Vidar struck him down, speedily avenging his father's death. Loki, with his wild-eyed face bereft of all reason, clambered over the dead and the dying, delighting in the destruction. He matched his fiery strength against the calm and controlled might of Heimdall. Swords crashed, sparks flew, cruel blades cut flesh, soon both gods lay dying from their many wounds.

The battle raged. Valkyrs were everywhere, riding hard upon their galloping steeds, urging the Einehar on against the relentless attacks of the army of giants. Bravely the warriors of Valhalla fought with no thoughts of victory, striving only to live their final moments of glory to the full. Their numbers dwindled, gods, men and giants fell by the score. Pained faces became calm as they greeted death's final release.

The battlefield became still. Corpses lay strewn in tangled webs of bloody flesh and shattered bone. Unseeing eyes stared out from cleft skulls. Hands clung in death to once cherished weapons, but their owners had little need of them. The fighting was over. Only Surtur the first born and the fire giants remained, standing on the battlefield's edge. Beyond them all was still. No sound, no movement, no bird or beast to feed upon the carrion; nothing to disturb the dead. Surtur passed his hand over the bloody field of death, spreading fire over the whole earth. All of creation was consumed by the flames.

a new heaven,
a new earth

In time the flames will die, and the universe will become cool once more. From the depths of the ocean a new earth will rise, with rich vegetation and fields of ripe golden grain. The daughter of the sun shall climb high into a clear blue sky and shine forth in greater splendour than her mother before her.

Throughout the destruction a woman named Lif and a man called Lifthrasir lay hidden within the World Tree. They will emerge and run in joy across the land. From them shall come a new race of men to live upon the earth.

Vidar and Vali will walk upon a new heaven unharmed by the ravages of the fire and flood. They will live upon the plain of Ida, where the realm of the gods once lay, and shall build a new Asgard far greater than before. To them shall come Modi and Magni bringing their father's hammer, Mjolnir, then Honir, and from the realm of the dead Hodur.

Finally, as radiant as the morning sun, Balder will return. Reborn in glory he will arrive to lead the gods in the new age. Together, and forever, they will rule over the new green earth.

the dwarfs

The dwarfs, the dark or black elves, lived in Svartalfheim. They originated from the maggots that grew in Ymir's fallen body which formed the earth. Living continually underground they found the bright light of the sun distasteful, and according to some traditions they were unable to come to the surface during the hours of day for fear of being turned to stone by the sun's rays. They were skilled workers of metals and manufacturered many of the gods' most precious possessions. Their names differed from place to place — in some areas they were called dwarfs and in others they were known as trolls.

the elves

The light or white elves lived in Alfheim and were ruled by the god Frey. Like their dark cousins the dwarfs, they were household spirits worshipped by ordinary folk in their own homes. Belief in their power far outlasted that of the gods, continuing into the Christian period, and existing until quite recent times. It may indeed still survive in more remote areas.

the giants

The giants were the oldest race in the universe, older than mankind and older than the gods. When Ymir, the first of the giants, was killed by the sons of Bor, the flood that issued forth drowned all the race of giants except for Bergelmir and his wife, who escaped in a dugout boat to set up home in Jotunheim. It was from these two that the later race of giants was descended.

the norns

The Norns governed the fate of both men and gods. They lived under the great ash tree Yggdrasil, near the pool of Urdar. Their names were Urd, Verdandi and Skuld, and they represented the past, present and future, respectively. Daily they would weave the web of fate, Urd and Verdandi working with care and skill, but their sister Skuld would undo their work, tearing it to shreds, representing the uncertainty of the future.

Urd was the oldest of the three, she looked constantly backwards into the past. Verdandi was young and active, seeing only in front of her. Skuld's eyes were covered by a veil; at times she held a closed book or tightly bound scroll.

the valkyrs

he Valkyrs were the warrior maids of Odin. They were the choosers of the slain. With the goddess Freya at their head they rode their horses down from Asgard and would gallop about the battlefield. With spears in their hands and shields upon their arms they wove in and out of the fighting men deciding who should live and who should die.

All who received their kiss of death were carried off to Valhalla. There the Einheriar, the fallen warriors, were treated as honoured guests. In a glorious never-ending banquet the Valkyrs waited upon them. They tended to the Einheriar's every need, supplying them with all the food they could eat and all the mead they could drink.

yggorasil

ggdrasil, the great World Ash, stood at the centre of the universe, its branches spreading wide to cover all the nine worlds while three great roots delve deep beneath the ground. The first root dipped into the inspirational waters of Mimir's spring — it was here that Heimdall rested his horn. The second root lay in the Well of Urd, where the Norns dwelt, weaving the fates of mankind and tending to the needs of the tree. The third root fell into the dark waters of Hvergelmir, where the dragon Nidghogg tore at corpses and knawed unceasingly at the tree.

Four stags nibbled hungrily at the tree's green buds, while goats tore at the bark. High in the branches an eagle sat with a hawk perched upon his brow. Between the eagle and the dragon a squirrel named Ratatosk scurried up and down the Ash all day conveying insults from one to the other.

Odin was wisest of all the gods, but to obtain his wisdom he had to make a great sacrifice. Journeying down amongst the roots of Yggdrasil, he sought and found Mimir's Well, the source of all knowledge, and there he asked to take a draught of the well's potent waters.

Mimir, who knew the power of the well, demanded an eye in return for granting Odin's request. Without a moment's hesitation, Odin plucked one eye from its socket and gave it gladly in exchange for the precious liquid. He drank deeply from Mimir's Well and received the wisdom he sought. That same time he reached up into the tree and broke off a branch which he fashioned into the spear Gungnir. It was with this spear that Odin chose to wound himself as he hung from the World Tree for nine nights and nine days. Suspended from the sacred tree he stared down into the deep waters.

Self-wounded and self-sacrificed he reached down, his tortured hand groping blindly in the dim light. Finally with a shout of triumph he grasped the great secret that he had longed for, the wisdom of the runes. He drew back in relief and joy, the knowledge was his at last.

Because of his experience upon Yggdrasil he came to be known as the lord of the gallows and the god of hanged men.

BiBLiOGRAPHY

Arbman, Holger, *The Vikings*, Thames & Hudson, London, 1962.

Auden, W.H. & Taylor, Paul B., *Norse Poems*, Faber and Faber, London, 1983.

Bosworth, Joseph, *Anglo-Saxon Dictionary*, John Russell Smith, London, 1852.

Branston, Brian, *Gods of the North*, Thames and Hudson, London, 1980.

—— *The Lost Gods of England*, Thames and Hudson, London, 1974.

Brown, David, *Anglo-Saxon England*, Bodley Head, London, 1978.

Bruce-Mitford, Rupert, *The Sutton Hoo Ship-Burial*, British Museum, London, 1972.

Chadwick, H.M., *The Cult of Othin*, C.J. Clay & Sons, London 1899.

Crossley-Holland, Kevin, *The Norse Myths*, Andre Deutsch, London, 1980.

Davison, H.R. Ellis, *Gods and Myths of Northern Europe*, Penguin, 1979.

—— *Scandinavian Mythology*, Paul Hamlyn, London, 1969.

Dronke, U. (ed), *The Poetic Edda*, Oxford University Press, London, 1969.

Elliot, Ralph W. V., *Runes: An Introduction*, Manchester University Press, Manchester, 1959.

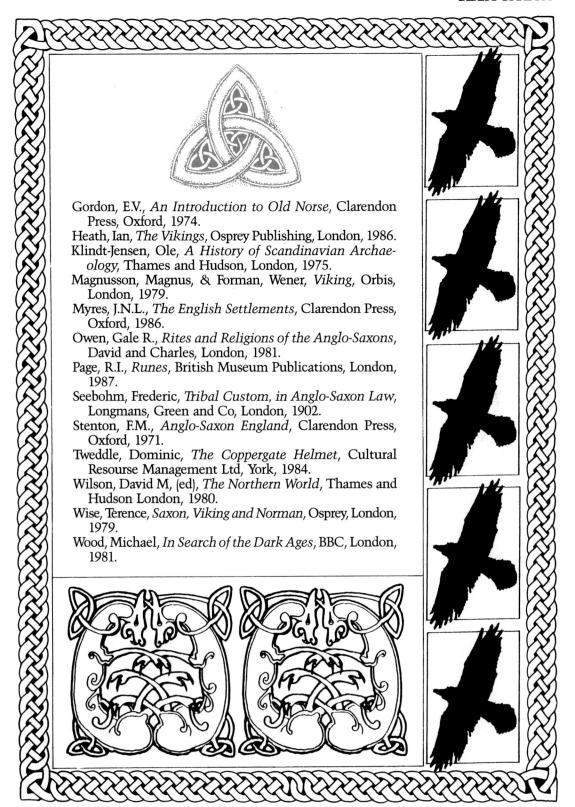

Gordon, E.V., *An Introduction to Old Norse*, Clarendon Press, Oxford, 1974.

Heath, Ian, *The Vikings*, Osprey Publishing, London, 1986.

Klindt-Jensen, Ole, *A History of Scandinavian Archaeology*, Thames and Hudson, London, 1975.

Magnusson, Magnus, & Forman, Wener, *Viking*, Orbis, London, 1979.

Myres, J.N.L., *The English Settlements*, Clarendon Press, Oxford, 1986.

Owen, Gale R., *Rites and Religions of the Anglo-Saxons*, David and Charles, London, 1981.

Page, R.I., *Runes*, British Museum Publications, London, 1987.

Seebohm, Frederic, *Tribal Custom, in Anglo-Saxon Law*, Longmans, Green and Co, London, 1902.

Stenton, F.M., *Anglo-Saxon England*, Clarendon Press, Oxford, 1971.

Tweddle, Dominic, *The Coppergate Helmet*, Cultural Resourse Management Ltd, York, 1984.

Wilson, David M, (ed), *The Northern World*, Thames and Hudson London, 1980.

Wise, Terence, *Saxon, Viking and Norman*, Osprey, London, 1979.

Wood, Michael, *In Search of the Dark Ages*, BBC, London, 1981.

índex

By the same author:

THE —

noRse
taRot

GODS, SAGAS AND RUNES FROM THE
—— LIVES OF THE VIKINGS ——

Clive Barrett

THE NORSE TAROT breaks new ground in Tarot conception. Skilfully combining strongly drawn figures with a beautifully subtle use of colour, artist and writer Clive Barrett has painted a deck of sheer beauty. And though carefully designed to correspond with traditional Tarot interpretations, the cards convey their meanings in a wholly original way and in a form consistent with the Nordic theme as a whole.

This special pack contains the outstanding Norse Tarot deck, together with a fully illustrated book which details the procedures needed to read them. In an absorbing introduction the author explains the history of the Viking peoples and their way of life and stresses the importance of their gods, sagas and rune figures in the construction of the Tarot cards. The interpretation of all 78 cards is given, and the historical and mythological background to the cards' images is lovingly explained.

THE NORSE TAROT will meet with great satisfaction from people of all walks of life: for the layman it offers a fascinating insight into the lives and beliefs of an archetypal race of warriors, with every card illustrating a fascinating story; for the novice it provides an incomparable introduction to the use of Tarot, complete with a basic guide to laying and reading the cards; and for the enthusiast who demands increasing quality if offers a highly original and imaginative new angle.